APPRENTICESHIPS

Business

Team Leader/ Supervisor

Handbook

LEVEL 3

Published by Pearson Education Limited, 80 Strand, London, WC2R 0RL.

www.pearsonschoolsandfecolleges.co.uk

Text © Pearson Education Limited
Edited by Just Content, Braintree, Essex
Typeset by PDQ Digital Media Solutions Ltd.
Original illustrations © Pearson Education Limited 2018
Picture research by Integra
Cover photo/illustration © office building windows: leungchopan / Shutterstock.com, four white light bulbs and one white one: fatido / Getty Images

The rights of Claire Parry and Julie Smith to be identified as authors of this work have been asserted by them in accordance with the Copyright, Designs and Patents Act 1988.

First published 2019

21 20 19
10 9 8 7 6 5 4 3 2 1

British Library Cataloguing in Publication Data
A catalogue record for this book is available from the British Library

ISBN 978 1 292 27991 6

Printed in Slovakia by Neografia

Acknowledgements

The author and publisher would like to thank the following individuals and organisations for permission to reproduce photographs:

123RF: 123RF 99, 125, bimdeedee 74, Dotshock 71, Everythingpossible 100, Ginasanders 139, Iculig 173, Marvent/Shutterstock 199, Andrey Popov 66, 89, pressmaster 37, Vadymvdrobot 86; **Pearson Education Ltd:** 32, 36, 40, 45, 48, 56, 58, 60, 65, 76, 80, 82, 85, 88, 95, 104, 105, 109, 112, 113, 114, 117, 126, 128, 130, 132, 134, 135, 144, 153, 159, 171, 172, 178, 188, 191, 201, 203, 205, 206, HBSS. Image Source 131, Debbie Rowe 23, happystock 6, Hurst Photo 7, Jules Selmes 68, Studio 8 4, 195; **Shutterstock:** Marcin Balcerzak 8, Fernando Batista 132, Blend Images 18, blurAZ 145, Fizkes 148, garagestock 173, Geo Martinez 3, imtmphoto 63, JohnKwan 163, Kheng Guan Toh 17, Lassedesignen 79, Rob Marmion 51, Mast3r 69, Stuart Miles 61, Monkey Business Images 1, 12 15, My Life Graphic 167, OtnaYdur 143, Paperboat 83, Pathdoc 52, Dusan Petkovic 81, David Pirvu 9, Pressmaster 165, Ivelin Radkov 41, Rawpixel 4, 22, 28, 90, Sam72 43, Shutterstock 157, 176, 185, 186, S.john 193, 195, Solis Images 2, SpeedKingz 154, wavebreakmedia 27.

Note from the publisher
Pearson has robust editorial processes, including answer and fact checks, to ensure the accuracy of the content in this publication, and every effort is made to ensure this publication is free of errors. We are, however, only human, and occasionally errors do occur. Pearson is not liable for any misunderstandings that arise as a result of errors in this publication, but it is our priority to ensure that the content is accurate. If you spot an error, please do contact us at resourcescorrections@pearson.com so we can make sure it is corrected.

Contents

About this book

This book is designed to support you through your on-programme learning as part of your apprenticeship for the *Team Leader/Supervisor Level 3* and as you prepare for your *end-point assessment (EPA)*. It is structured around the standards for the apprenticeship while all the information comes from the essential knowledge for the mandatory units. While you work through the book you will see it highlights the attitudes, values and behaviours that you will need to demonstrate in your day-to-day work.

Practical help for you in your role

Although this book will help you in your studies, and through your learning journey as an apprentice, it is also designed to help you in a practical way. All the activities and examples are taken from a range of team leader/supervisor skills and feature different roles so that you can relate them to your own experiences and learn to grow within your job role – and particularly in taking on the Level 3 role. We hope you will be able to use the book as a professional tool long after you have gained your apprenticeship.

How to use this book

This book has been designed and structured around the Apprenticeship Standard. There are pages that cover the knowledge 'what you must know and understand' and the skills you will need to put that knowledge in place 'what you must be able to do'.

In this way you will be able to see how what you *do* relates to what you *know* – and the other way around.

Features of the book

To make your learning easier and to help you prepare for your EPA this is what we have provided:

Introduction to the start of each section to explain what is covered.

 Summary text to help you focus on what you need to know.

 Key terms – important words are highlighted and defined so you know how to use them in the context of your work. The first time they appear in the book they will be explained. If you can't quite remember the definition look in the Glossary afterwards. They are all listed there.

 Activity – a range of different activities helping you put your knowledge into practice.

 Links to Standard – so you know how the information and activities in the book relate Team Leader/Supervisor apprenticeship.

Topic consolidation Topic consolidation – this will help you to make sense of your work and review your understanding to help you develop in your role.

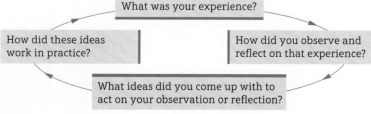

The Kolb learning cycle

Specific help for your end-point assessment

Throughout your programme, you will have been gathering evidence from work activities so that you can demonstrate your knowledge, skills and behaviour in your Team Leader/Supervisor role. All of these will have been reviewed and you will have been given feedback to assist you in the final preparation for the EPA.

Your end-point assessment is the opportunity for you to show what you have learnt.

Component 1: Multiple-choice test

Component 2: Portfolio of evidence

Component 3: Competency-based interview

Component 4: Professional discussion

The multiple choice test is an on-screen test that will assess your underpinning knowledge and your knowledge of the skills required across the Apprenticeship Standard. The test consists of some short scenarios together with multi-choice questions and only one right answer.

The portfolio of evidence is a collection of samples of work-based evidence that you have produced. This should demonstrate the knowledge, skills and behaviours you have used to carry out your work competently. Any evidence you include in your portfolio must be naturally occurring from your work activities over the duration of your apprenticeship.

The competency-based interview is a planned, structured competence-based discussion between you and the independent end-point assessor. The primary purpose of the interview is to assess your ability to apply your understanding of the seven knowledge areas of the Apprenticeship Standard in carrying out your role as Team Leader/Supervisor.

Professional discussion is a planned, structured discussion between you and the independent end-point assessor. The primary purpose of the professional discussion is to assess how well you have managed your continuing professional development (CPD) during the course of your apprenticeship.

For the full end-point assessment evidence requirements, please refer to the Pearson Level 3 end-point assessment for Team Leader/Supervisor specification.

Tips to help you during the Competency Based Interview and Professional Discussion

Key tips

- Speak slowly and clearly – do not interrupt or talk over the other person.

- Listen carefully to questions. Do not be afraid to ask for something to be repeated if you do not hear or understand – do not let your attention drift.

- Avoid jargon or acronyms as your listener may not understand.

- Ask yourself questions as you listen in case you need to clarify anything.

- Take notes if this helps you – in case you need to revisit a point.

- **Be confident – you've done a great job so far to get to this stage.**

About the authors

Claire Parry

Claire has 20 years of experience working in education and training across the business sector. As an experienced assessor, she has worked with a range of learners and apprentices across the sector, preparing them for employment and assisting them to be successful in assessment.

Claire is also an established author, writing books and educational resources for a range of business-related programmes.

Julie Smith

Starting her career in the travel industry, Julie has since undertaken a number of managerial and leading roles, within this industry and in education. As a qualified teacher and assessor, Julie has spent several years teaching at further education colleges across Somerset and has also worked in the training departments of commercial enterprises.

More recently she has been involved in the delivery of apprenticeship programmes for Team Leading currently leads a team of Pearson External Quality Assurer's. In addition, she runs her own business, leading and directing a team of people and delivering a number of educational courses.

1
Leadership styles

The way in which a leader manages their team is likely to depend on their own skills set and the way in which they interact with people. Everyone is unique, and individuals will behave in different ways according to the position or task in hand. There are three areas you should think about when considering which leadership style you are likely to be more comfortable with:

- how you deal with people
- how you manage the work to be done
- how you see your own role.

The four leadership styles

The context and situation you find yourself in is likely to determine the most appropriate leadership style for you to adopt. Table 1 shows the four leadership styles. Each leadership style has its own characteristics that can have a negative or positive impact on your team. The leadership style will, in turn, have an impact on the results of your team and their success.

It is the skill of the team leader to know when to use the most appropriate leadership style, or combination of styles. This ensures they keep their **subordinates** engaged, so that the whole team will be effective in achieving their goals.

How do you view your role as a team leader?

The four leadership styles
Autocratic
Paternalistic
Democratic
Laissez-faire

Table 1: Which style of leadership do you naturally lean towards?

The autocratic leader

The autocratic leader holds the power within their team and will supervise them directly. They tend to use a top-down style of leading where they tell their team what to do rather than consult with them; see table 2. They tend not to **delegate**.

Using this style of leadership works well when managing new or untrained team members who may not know what tasks to perform or which procedures to follow. For example, a new team member in their first month will probably need to be told what is required of them and be closely managed by their team leader as they learn about the company and their job role.

How would you react to the autocratic style of leadership?

It can also be an effective style of leadership when directing and focusing a multi-skilled team or if there is a need for urgent action, such as getting a job done in a very short time.

Link to the standard

Knowledge Area 1: Outcome Topic 1.1

Key term

Delegate – Trust someone to do a job for you.

Behaviours B

Takes responsibility – Determination when managing difficult situations.

Positive impacts	Negative impacts
Allows for quick decision-making	Can demoralise team members
Can increase productivity and quality	Can create environment of fear and/or mistrust
Can reduce inefficiencies	High staff turnover or absenteeism
Good to use in dangerous situations	Can stifle creativity

Table 2: How would you use the autocratic leadership style?

The paternalistic leader

This type of leadership implies a similar relationship to that between a parent and child. The leader will make all of the decisions in the best interests of the team members' welfare and needs, with very little consultation or delegation. Under this style of leadership the team members will follow the direction of the leader.

The paternalistic style of leadership works well with less experienced or confident team members and in organisations where there is a formal and hierarchical structure. For example, when a team member is lacking in confidence they are likely to feel comfortable when their team leader makes decisions on their behalf. They will feel secure and supported when led in this way. This can lead to a positive relationship with their team leader, as shown in table 3.

How would you react to the paternalistic style of leadership?

Positive impacts	Negative impacts
Will gain trust and loyalty from team	Can restrict creativity and individualism
Employee retention is good	Little team empowerment
Positive relationship between team and team leader	Team will become dependent on the team leader
Team motivation is likely to be good	Likely to demotivate experienced team members

Table 3: In which situation would you use the paternalistic leadership style?

The democratic leader

The democratic leader shares the power and decision-making with their team through regular consultation and delegation. They use open debate and encourage the team to share their ideas in the planning stage of a project or in solving any problems. There is a great deal of flexibility in the democratic leadership style that can lead to a better way of doing things and it can bring out the best in an experienced and motivated team. However, the democratic leader will make the final decision, based on team discussions and with the majority view of the team on the best course of action, which can slow down the decision-making process.

This style of leadership can be very effective when there is a large or complex problem to solve or when encouraging team-building and full participation from each member of the team. For example, if a team leader has been asked to come up with a new advertising campaign, they can use the democratic leadership style with the team, to encourage a creative environment where team members can come up with new ideas and **innovations**. These can be explored and discussed before any final decisions are made; see table 4.

Key term

Innovation – A new and creative idea, device or process.

Link to the standard

Knowledge Area 1: Outcome Topic 1.1

How would you react to the democratic style of leadership?

Positive impacts	Negative impacts
High job satisfaction with the team and morale	Leader is seen as weak
High team productivity	Can slow up the decision-making process
Encourages creativity and innovation	Decisions are based on compromise
Team members will get personal and professional development	There is a potential for communication failure and incomplete projects

Table 4: How would you use the democratic leadership style in your role?

The laissez-faire leader

The laissez-faire leader uses a high level of delegation, trusting the team to make their own decisions. The team therefore hold the power. The leader will provide guidance and support to their team, checking results, but not interfering. However there will be a high level of **autonomy** as team members have the freedom to undertake their work.

This style of leadership works well with skilled and experienced teams, when they are highly motivated and able to work independently, take responsibility and are not afraid to make decisions. For example, a recently appointed team leader joining an existing experienced and skilled team can use the laissez-faire style of leadership while getting to know the team by letting them work independently while they observe from a distance. This is a good way to see how the team progresses and to know exactly what they are capable of, while determining the different characters within the team; see table 5.

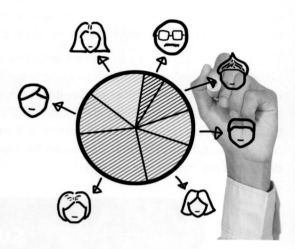

How do you delegate to your team?

Positive impacts	Negative impacts
Can lead to high job satisfaction	Team leader can have a poor role definition
Can lead to high team morale	Potential for low productivity
Empowers the team and the individuals within the team	Can lead to a lack of commitment within the team
Can increase team and individuals' confidence	Can lead to individuals within the team not taking responsibility for their actions

Table 5: How would you react to the laissez-faire style of leadership?

Adjusting leadership styles

Within your team you are likely to have a wide range of ability and experience across the individual team members. By using the four different leadership styles, you can adapt and adjust your style to suit the individual within the team as well as the whole team. There are also outside influences that are likely to affect the way you lead your team and the way your team behave.

Be aware of the business environment

Learn to work with and embrace uncertainty that your working environment may bring. By encouraging your team to look for new approaches and be comfortable with change, they can look for solutions to achieve the company's goals and reach their own potential. Look at any difficult situations with a different perspective; it may be that you need to forget existing procedures and create new ones to respond to the wider business context. Inspire your team to use their best skills in order to find creative solutions.

Leading with empathy

Think about how outside organisations might see your own organisation, so that you can communicate this to your own team. In response to this, listen to your own team members' ideas and see things from their point of view. Give them autonomy, so that they can focus on achieving rather than completing individual tasks.

Leading through correction and reflection

There may be times when you will need to try out things that don't succeed. These experiences will be useful if you reflect and learn from them by understanding what went wrong and what can be done differently to avoid the situation arising again. Involve your team in this correction and reflection process, allowing them to make decisions to take things forward.

Creating win-win situations

There are likely to be a number of interested parties to consider that you should make your team aware of. By involving your team and getting them to understand the needs of customers and other key **stakeholders**, such as suppliers, you can work towards a win-win situation.

Key terms

Empathy – Understand the feelings of a team member, without feeling sorry for them.

Stakeholder – Any person who has an interest in your business or business activities.

Link to the standard

Knowledge Area 1: Outcome Topic 1.1

Behaviours

Takes responsibility – Demonstrates resilience and accountability.

Agile – Flexible to the needs of the organisation; positive and adaptable.

How can you encourage win-win situations with your team?

Summary

This section has been about using different leadership styles and approaches:
- the four different leadership styles and when to use them
- their negative and positive impacts
- the need to adjust and adapt when using these leadership styles.

Benefits of coaching

Coaching is a process which usually involves one-to-one discussion and support aimed at helping a person to improve and maximise their performance. Effective coaching will equip individuals with the tools, knowledge and opportunities they need to develop themselves through self-exploration of a situation and what needs to be achieved.

Key term

Needs analysis – A process to establish the training and/or development needs of an individual.

Link to the standard

Knowledge Area 1: Outcome Topic 1.2

How does coaching benefit team members?

Workplace coaching starts with a **needs analysis** of an individual through self-assessment. Used effectively, coaching will lead to on-the-job learning, which should be tailored to the needs of the individual, building on their existing knowledge and experience. A structured approach to learning is used in the coaching process while allowing for flexibility in its delivery. Measurable learning and performance targets can be identified and achieved adding value to the individual and their organisation.

GROW model

The GROW model was developed in the 1980s by Graham Alexander, Alan Fine and John Whitmore; see table 6. The intention of the GROW model is that the coach acts as a **facilitator,** helping the **coachee** select the best options for them rather than offering advice or direction. The coach does not need to have expert knowledge, but rather has to be a good listener, who can take the coachee through a series of steps in recognising what they need to achieve and how they will achieve it. However, as a team leader you are likely to have the expert knowledge and so you will be able to guide your team member to make decisions that are best for them and for your organisation.

Link to the standard

Knowledge Area 1: Outcome Topic 1.2

Key terms

Facilitator – A person who helps another find an answer to a problem or to do something more easily through guidance or supervision.

Coachee – This is the individual being coached.

Behaviours   B

Professionalism – Operates within organisational values.

The model	How do you use it?
Goal	The first stage is for you to guide your team member towards identifying their goal. What is it that they wish to achieve? How will they know that their goal has been achieved? How does the goal fit in with the team member's personal development plan (PDP) or career objectives? Does it fit in with the team's and organisation's values and objectives?
Reality	Your role at this stage is to help your team member recognise their current reality rather than tell them. If they find this difficult, you can help them by asking probing questions such as 'what is happening now?', 'have you taken any steps towards your goal?' or 'does this goal conflict with anything else?'.
Options	The next stage is to encourage your team member to explore all of the options available to them. You can offer suggestions; however, you should let your team member come up with their own. Discussion can then help your team member decide which options to pursue.
Way forward	The final stage is for your team member to consider the next steps. SMART objectives should be set based on the goals established and the options available, then a plan of action can be made. You can guide and support your team member in creating the action plan; however, they should be encouraged to decide on the actions agreed and write up their own plan.

Table 6: Think of a way that you could use the GROW model within your team

What elements of your own training would you reuse with others?

CLEAR model

Similar to the GROW model, the CLEAR model was created in the 1980s by Peter Hawkins; see table 7.

Key term

Ground rules – Principles of behaviours and actions that both parties agree to.

The model	How do you use it?
Contract	During the initial discussion with your team member, establish how the coaching will be undertaken. Agree the **ground rules**, ensuring that you are both open and honest. Help your team member to set the outcomes they wish to achieve.
Listen	Actively listen to your team member so that you can understand their situation.
Explore	Through discussion, help your team member to understand any impact their current situation may be having on them. You can then challenge your team member to think through possible resolutions.
Action	Guide your team member in deciding how they are going to progress following the discussion. Encourage them to write up an action plan with deadlines. It is good practice to keep a copy of the action plan for your own records.
Review	Review what you have covered during the coaching meeting. Confirm what was discussed and ask your team member for feedback on how the coaching session has helped them. Find out if there is anything they would like to do differently next time and what they liked about the session.

Table 7: What additional steps are included in the CLEAR model?

Behaviours B

Professionalism – Open and honest.

FUEL model

Developed by John Zenger and Kathleen Stinnett, the FUEL model is based on the coach asking open and non-leading questions to guide the conversation with the coachee; see table 8. Using this approach, it allows the individual to come up with their own solutions and take ownership of the coaching process and accountability for the outcome.

Behaviours B

Professionalism – Sets an example, and is fair, consistent and impartial.

The model	How do you use it?
Frame the conversation	Your initial focus should be on what your team member wishes to achieve. Agree on the purpose of the coaching, the process and what the outcomes will be.
Understand the current state	Guide your team member into understanding what their current situation is. Ask questions throughout the discussion so that you can see things from their perspective. Be consistent and impartial during the discussions.
Explore the desired state	The next step is to help your team member think about where they would like to be at the end of the coaching sessions, i.e. their desired state. You should help them through discussion to generate different and alternative paths to get to this desired state.
Lay out a plan for success	The final stage is to create an action plan with SMART outcomes. Ensure that your team member draws up an action plan and on it, details the desired outcomes with the specific steps they will need to be take in order to achieve it.

Table 8: Would you use different coaching models with different team members?

Planning coaching sessions

Planning is key to a successful coaching session, regardless of which model you use. You should plan each session taking the following into consideration:

- the development needs of your team member against those of the organisation.
- the agreed aims and objectives
- the needs and ability of the team member you are coaching
- any resources that may be required during the coaching sessions and to support your team member between sessions
- any requirements, such as health and safety, and how this will be implemented.
- identifying and developing activities to achieve the coaching objectives
- planning for any contingencies for when things don't go to plan.

Finally, with your team member, draw up a coaching plan for you to refer to and update as necessary.

The coaching plan

The purpose of a coaching plan is to put in writing what all parties have agreed to for the duration of the coaching sessions; see table 9. It acts as a reminder of what is to be achieved as well as a record of when these achievements are met. A plan similar to the one shown in table 9 can then be used to reflect on how effective the coaching has been.

Objective	How will this be achieved?	Resources required?	Who will be responsible?	What are the success measures?	Target date

Table 9: Research your organisation's coaching plans

Behaviours

Inclusive – Open, approachable, authentic, and able to build trust with others.

Professionalism – Open and honest. Operates within organisational values.

Link to the standard

Interpersonal Excellence Skills Area 1: leading people

Giving feedback

The way in which you give feedback to those you coach is important to ensure your feedback is supportive and fair. When giving feedback, ensure you are in a quiet location where you will not be disturbed and where you cannot be overheard.

Table 10 shows the BOOST model in giving feedback.

The model	How do you use it?
Balanced	Focus on your team member's strengths and the areas that require development. When giving feedback on negative points, turn this into developmental feedback by including constructive points on how their performance and development can be improved.
Observed	Base your feedback on what you have observed rather than on what you think or what you feel.
Objective	Base your feedback on facts, actions and outcomes. Never on the personality of your team member.
Specific	Back up your comments with specific examples from what you have observed whether giving positive or developmental feedback. Even when team members have performed well, say what they did well.
Timely	Give your feedback as soon as possible so that you capture what you have observed and are able to feed back as accurately as possible.

Table 10: How could you use the BOOST model of feedback?

Individual learning styles

The VAK (Visual (seeing), Auditory (hearing), Kinaesthetic (doing)) learning styles model was developed in the 1920s. These three styles of learning identified the ways in which people learn, through seeing, hearing or doing.

Neil D Fleming added reading and writing to the model to create the VARK learning styles model. Most people use a combination of these learning styles, depending on what they are learning and in which context or situation.

Visual

Those with a visual preference are likely to learn and absorb more if information is presented through visual **mediums** such as pictures, diagrams and charts.

Auditory

Listening to instructions or taking part in group discussion is the preferred medium to learn or take in information when a team member has an auditory preference.

Kinaesthetic

A hands-on approach is preferred by those with a kinaesthetic preference. They learn and absorb information best of all when they can physically experience what they are learning.

Reading and writing

Repetition of words through reading and writing is what this team member will prefer. They are likely to take down notes and read them through later to help them digest and take in information.

What style of learning is taking place?

Managing change through coaching

There are several changes that can happen within your organisation that may affect your team, such as changes in policies and procedure, organisational restructuring, changing your range of products or services or even moving location; see table 11.

When these changes occur, it is important that your team understand the reasons why and how these changes might affect them. As the team leader, it is important that you identify any potential impact change is likely to have on your team members and team as a whole, both negative and positive. You will then be in a position to identify any potential barriers so that you can work out a way of overcoming them.

Overcoming barrier to change	Managing the team through change	Providing effective leadership through change
Inform and educate your team.	Use relevant project management tools and hold people accountable to ensure timely completion of tasks.	Create a positive and professional environment.
Provide a clear vision.	Communicate the **rationale** and benefits of any change.	Engage and empower your team members throughout the change.
Create a climate that engages people to become involved so that they contribute.	Create and then share your change management plan allocating and delegating tasks to enable team members to drive the change.	Recognise your team members' feelings and manage them effectively.
Establish clear processes so that ideas and suggestions can be generated.	Manage team expectations and monitor barriers ensuring action is taken to overcome these barriers as appropriate.	Demonstrate empathy and **emotional intelligence** when supporting team members.

Table 11: Overcoming barriers to change

Link to the standard

Skills Area 1:
Outcome Topic 1.2

Behaviours B

Takes responsibility – Determination when managing difficult situations.

Inclusive – Open, approachable, authentic, and able to build trust with others.

Agile – Responds well to feedback and need for change.

Key terms

Rationale – Reasons or a logical basis for a course of actions.

Emotional intelligence – Being aware of and able to express your emotions while controlling them effectively.

Summary

In this section you have learned about the benefits of coaching and the skills you need in order to support and improve the performance of your team members. This section has covered:

- definition and benefits of coaching
- GROW, CLEAR and FUEL models to use while coaching
- planning coaching sessions
- giving feedback
- VAK learning styles and preferences to be aware of while coaching
- managing change through coaching.

Organisational cultures

Your organisation will have developed and shaped its own **organisational culture** that in turn will influence the way individuals behave. Boundaries will have been set to reflect the values of your company and it is important that you and your team understand your organisational culture in order to be successful and to give employees a sense of direction.

There are internal and external factors that can have an effect on organisational culture as well as internal and external stakeholders, who can have an impact on and help to shape an organisational culture.

Internal influences

Individuals who have worked within an organisation for many years may have a large influence on its culture. Newer members of staff may find it difficult to change mentalities, interests and even thought processes. There are lots of other historical factors that can influence a culture, such as the customer base, nature of the business and style of management.

Primary function

The culture of an organisation will depend greatly on its primary function. For example, if there is a need for attention to detail, such as in an accountancy firm, the culture is likely to be very different to that of a company driven by outcomes and results where processes are less important. It is different again in an organisation where the focus is on people, such as an activity centre, where the culture is based on the well-being and safety of the staff and customers.

Size Senior managers or owners of small companies are likely to be closer to their staff and therefore have a greater impact on the culture. In larger organisations, where management is larger and more structured, the culture is likely to have a greater corporate atmosphere. In both cases, individuals have an influence on its culture, therefore the greater the number of staff, the more the culture may be diluted.

Location This can influence the culture of an organisation, and whether it has a local or national presence.

Technology Most organisations will use technology and some will be totally dependent on it. This may affect the way in which staff members communicate and work with each other and their customers. For example, an international online retailer may use emails and electronic communications with staff and customers and won't actively encourage face-to-face interaction. Other organisations, such as a veterinary practice, may use technology to support the management of the business, but the culture is to have a hands-on and personal interaction with its customers.

What are the internal influencers in your organisation?

Organisational goals Strategies and procedures are created by organisations to meet their goals and targets influence their culture. For example, those working for government or local council departments will be required to follow set guidelines and procedures to ensure deadlines and goals are met. However, an advertising firm is likely to expect its staff to be autonomous in their decision-making and creativity, in order to meet their deadlines and goals.

Management and staff The way in which management treats their employees will have a great impact and influence on its culture. A business that allows its employees to be part of the decision-making process will be very different to one that closely manages its employees and expects them to always follow instructions. Employees who view their job as a means to just make money are more likely to change jobs frequently. This has a negative impact on the culture and should be avoided where possible.

Key term

Demographics –
Statistical data relating to
particular groups within
the population.

**Link to the
standard**

Knowledge Area 1:
Outcome Topic 1.3

Behaviours

Agile – Is creative,
innovative and
enterprising when
seeking solutions to
business needs. Positive
and adaptable, responds
well to feedback and need
for change.

External influences

The external influences likely to have an effect on an organisation can be identified through a PESTLE analysis where an organisation can determine how each factor will affect the performance and activities of its business; see table 12 . How this is managed can have a positive or negative impact on an organisation's culture.

PESTLE	How can it influence an organisation's culture?
Political	This refers to government policies, laws, taxes, regulations and any other interventions that may be introduced by the government affecting organisations. For example, new government legislation in age equality relating to retirement age could lead to a change of culture as the age **demographics** within the organisation change.
Economic	Economic factors include interest rates, exchange rates and inflation. These impact on the disposable income available to employees and customers of an organisation. For example, an organisation affected by high interest rates may need to cut employee hours. This could positively impact a culture where staff pull together to ensure the success of the organisation, or it may adversely impact a culture if employees are earning less.
Social	Social factors include educational requirements or changing career attitudes to the workforce. For example, an organisation whose culture is focused on staff development is likely to sponsor training courses and encourage career progression creating a culture of growth within the organisation.
Technological	As technology advances, organisations need to embrace the changes to ensure they remain competitive in their field. The impact can be seen when an organisation changes from manual to electronic systems and processes or implements new technology.
Legal	This refers to laws such as Discrimination, Health and Safety, Consumer Protection, Copyright, Patent, Data Protection, etc. that an organisation must comply with . This may mean that systems and processes require regulation, and any changes to ensure a business is compliant can lead to a shift in culture.
Environmental	Different organisations have different approaches to how they manage their impact on the environment. As organisations become more responsible and change their policies, this is likely to have an impact on their culture.

Table 12: What external influences impact your organisation?

Functional cultures of stakeholders Any stakeholders, internal or external, who have an interest in an organisation can also influence its culture. These stakeholders may have their own cultural values that may not reflect those of the organisation. This imbalance or potential clash of cultures can impact on the organisational culture.

Internal stakeholders These are likely to be business owners, managers and the staff within the organisation.

External stakeholders These are likely to be customers, suppliers, employer or employee bodies, the local community or the government.

Behaviours

Professionalism – Operates within organisational values.

Who are the key stakeholders influencing the culture in your organisation?

Handy's types of organisational culture

Charles Handy defined four different kinds of culture: power, role, task and person. Table 13 explains how each one has its own characteristics and impacts and influences team members.

Kind of culture	Characteristic	Positive impact and influence on team members	Negative impact and influence on team members
Power	There will be few rules and regulations. Employees are judged by what they achieve rather than how they do things. Autocratic leadership and hierarchical structures are common in organisations with a power culture.	Individuals' talents and skills can be utilised.	It can lead to staff dissatisfaction, conflict and under-utilisation of creativity and initiatives. Lower-level managers or team members may be afraid of communicating bad news to the leader.

Link to the standard

Knowledge Area 1: Outcome Topic 1.3

Role	The culture is based on rules, which staff will operate within and where little creativity is shown. The organisation structure is well defined and everyone knows their roles and responsibilities. Power is determined by a person's position within the organisation.	This role offers security and the opportunity to acquire specialist expertise. Performance up to a required standard is rewarded on the appropriate pay-scale and possible promotion within the department.	Decision-making can be slow and risk-taking is discouraged. It can be frustrating for ambitious people who are power-orientated, want control over their work or are more interested in results than method.
Task	Teams are empowered to take decisions and are often formed to address specific problems or to progress projects. Team members are encouraged to be creative and there may be a strong spirit within the team, which can lead to a very motivating environment.	There is a high degree of autonomy and team members are judged by results. There are good relationships within the teams and a mutual respect based on ability.	Individual performances or initiatives may not be recognised, leading to possible negative implications for the level of motivation of individuals. There is a possibility that personal relationship issues may stand in the way of productivity within the team.
Person	The organisation exists in order for people to work and individuals can see themselves as unique and superior to the organisation. Can become a collection of individuals who happen to work for the same organisation.	Individuals are usually experts in their fields and their expertise is valued. They do like to work alone. Suits individuals who find it difficult to work effectively in a more structured organisation.	Because individuals like to work alone they can have little respect for organisational systems and processes.

Table 13: Handy's types of organisational culture

Which of Handy's four styles is closest to your own organisation's culture?

Techniques to use in influencing a team culture

Create a clear vision

1. Set aside time to think about what you want your team to do.

2. Visualise the reality of what you want to achieve.

3. Create an environment that will help you succeed.

4. Be clear about your values and what you expect from your team.

Be a role model by:

1. demonstrating confidence

2. showing respect and concern for others

3. being knowledgeable

4. admitting to your mistakes.

Encourage appropriate team behaviour that:

1. aligns to your organisation's culture

2. creates consistency across your team

3. encourages new and creative ideas

4. encourages openness and honesty.

Be inclusive by:

1. respecting the values of your team members

2. recognising team members' goals

3. rewarding appropriate attitude.

4. understanding when team members are making assumptions.

Build mutual respect and understanding

1. Treat everyone in your team with courtesy.

2. Be aware of your non-verbal communication.

3. Encourage your team to express their opinions and ideas.

4. Listen to your team members before expressing your viewpoint.

Behaviours	B

Takes responsibility – Demonstrates resilience and accountability.

Inclusive – Able to build trust with others. Seeks views of others.

Agile – Is creative, innovative and enterprising when seeking solutions to business needs. Positive and adaptable, responds well to feedback and need for change.

Summary

This section is about organisational cultures and how they can be influenced through different styles. You have learned about:

- internal and external influences and the impact they can have on an organisation's culture
- the internal and external stakeholders that affect organisational culture
- Handy's types of organisational culture, the characteristics of the four types and the impact each can have on an organisation's culture
- the techniques you can use as a team leader to influence your team's culture.

Equality and diversity

Behaviours

Inclusive – Open, approachable, authentic, and able to build trust with others.

Professionalism – Sets an example, and is fair, consistent and impartial.

Link to the standard

Knowledge Area 1: Outcome Topic 1.4

Equality and diversity will impact across many operational policies within your organisation and it is important that you understand how they specifically affect those policies that most closely align with your working role and responsibilities.

As a team leader you need to consider how you can ensure equality of opportunity in employment, pay and promotion and embrace diversity through valuing individual differences, including lifestyles, cultures, ethnicity, religion and gender.

You should promote an inclusive environment within your team where respect and acceptance of individuals is a part of the culture and expected behaviour. You should act then necessary to ensure all team members consider each other's differences.

The Equality Act 2010 specifically protects employees against discrimination in relation to:

- dismissal – being sacked or removed from your job

- employment terms and conditions – contractual details such as hours worked, shift patterns

- pay and benefits – equal wages, pension contributions, sick pay, etc.

- training – access to educational courses and continual professional development, etc.

- recruitment – how an organisation attracts, screens and selects applicants for a job

- redundancy – when someone is dismissed because their job is no longer needed.

It is unlawful to face discrimination in any of these circumstances because of defined protected personal characteristics set out within the Equality Act 2010.

The nine protected characteristics are set out in table 14.

Protected Characteristic	What this means
Age	Employees may need protecting because they are younger or older than a comparable employee. For example, organisations cannot put an age restriction on a staff development programme; it must be open to the whole of the workforce.
Disability	Employees may need protecting because of a learning difficulty. For example, an organisation cannot pay an individual less to do a job because they are dyslexic.
Gender reassignment	Employees may need protecting due to gender reassignment. Someone undergoing the process to change gender should be referred to as a transsexual. Being absent from work for such surgery must not be treated differently to any other medical procedure.
Marriage and civil partnership	Employees may need protection because of their married or civil partnership status. No employee should be discriminated against because of their marital status.
Pregnancy and maternity	Employees may need protection because of pregnancy. For example, an employer cannot take pregnancy related illness into account when calculating an individual's level of general sickness absence.
Race	Employees may need protection because of their race. Typically this term includes a combination of different elements, colour, ethnic or national origin and nationality. Someone from another country must not be subject to racial slurs.
Religion	Employees may need protection because of their religion or philosophical belief. For example, workplace adjustments and respect for important religious holidays should be applied fairly to all team members.
Sex	Employees may need protection because of their sex (gender). For example, managers should not favour individuals of a particular gender and all employees should be protected from verbal or physical sexual harassment, including displays of offensive material.
Sexual orientation	Employees may need protection because of their sexual orientation. No one should be bullied because they are, or are perceived to be, gay, lesbian, bisexual or heterosexual.

Table 14: The nine protected characteristics

Link to the standard

Knowledge Area 1: Outcome Topic 1.4

Behaviours

Inclusive – Open, approachable, authentic, and able to build trust with others.

Professionalism – Sets an example, and is fair, consistent and impartial.

Forms of discrimination and harassment

Direct discrimination

Direct discrimination happens when a team member is treated less favourably because of a protected characteristic. It could also be due to a protected characteristic of someone with whom they are associated, such as a family member. This is direct discrimination by association.

It is also possible to directly discriminate by perception. In other words, a team member thought to have a protected characteristic, regardless of whether they have it or not.

Indirect discrimination

Indirect discrimination is often not recognised and can be unintended. It can happen when a working provision or practice is applied equally to a group of employees or job applicants, but it actually creates a particular disadvantage for those who share a certain protected characteristic compared to others in the group.

Harassment

Harassment is unwanted behaviour towards an individual that relates directly to a relevant protected characteristic. It typically violates a person's dignity or intimidates, degrades, humiliates or is offensive. Harassment includes basic sexist behaviour, bullying, persona jokes, inappropriate banter, gossip, etc. It can also include insults or unwanted verbal, written or physical contact and is based on the victim's perception rather than that of the **perpetrator.**

Victimisation

Victimisation occurs when an employee is treated less favourably than others due to making a formal complaint, grievance or allegation of discrimination. It can also occur through association when supporting another complainant alleging discrimination or providing evidence or witness testimony for such cases. Victimisation may also happen when an employee is only perceived to be doing these things.

How do you ensure you are meeting the equality and diversity requirements within your organisation?

Employer responsibilities and liabilities

An employer must inform all staff of the legal requirements for equality and diversity and make regular checks to ensure that all employees are **adhering** to the organisational policies. Staff training on equality and diversity must also be provided. Reasonable adjustments must also be made by the employer to remove barriers for people with disabilities. For example, a disabled worker could be provided with a nearby parking space or a team member who has back pain could be given a posture chair.

An employer is legally responsible for acts of discrimination, harassment and victimisation carried out by their employees, regardless of whether they are aware of any such behaviours. They must investigate and act in response to any discrimination and harassment complaints. If an employer can prove that they have taken all reasonable preventative actions, then they will not be legally responsible. It is therefore important that any complaints or potential situations that could lead to discrimination are investigated and actions written down and recorded.

Key term

Adhering – Follow and be in support of something.

Link to the standard

Knowledge Area 1: Outcome Topic 1.4

How do you make sure your organisation has provided reasonable adjustments?

| Behaviours | B |

Inclusive – Open, approachable, authentic, and able to build trust with others.

Professionalism – Operates within organisational values.

Your own personal behaviour

As a team leader, you should display appropriate personal behaviour, acting as a role model and using communication styles appropriate to different people and different situations. Be aware of the language you use, ensuring it is non-discriminatory and allow others to express views, which may be different to your own. Show respect for the backgrounds of individuals, their values, beliefs and customs, so that you are fair and consistent in your decision-making. You will then start to see the benefits of equality and diversity as it promotes a culture of inclusion and respect, which is then likely to improve team working and increase productivity.

Another benefit of equality and diversity is that barriers to recruitment and progression are removed and it is likely to attract and retain staff with a number of different talents and competencies.

Summary

In this section, you have learnt about the different aspects of equality and diversity, including:
- Equality Act 2010
- the nine protected characteristics
- employers responsibilities and liabilities
- your personal behaviour and responsibilities
- the benefits of equality and diversity.

Activities

▶ Activity 1

Think about your own skills and ways of working and how these fit with the four different styles of leadership by answering the following questions:

How do you deal with people?

How do you manage the workflow within your team?

How do you see your role as a team leader?

▶ Activity 2

Have a discussion with your manager or tutor to get their assessment of your skills and ways of working. Identify which styles of leader you naturally lean towards and which styles you need to work on.

▶ Activity 3

Draw up an action plan, based on your self-reflection and feedback from your manager or tutor, of how you can improve the skills required to be flexible when using the different styles of leadership.

▶ Activity 4

Using one of the three different models of coaching: GOAL, CLEAR and FUEL, plan to undertake a coaching session with one of your team where you need to manage a change.

What preparations will you need to undertake, including yourself or any materials/equipment?

Identify the change and any possible barriers to the change.

Create and implement a coaching plan to use with your team member that demonstrates how you have managed the change and provided effective leadership through the coaching session or sessions.

▶ Activity 5

Find out about the culture of your organisation and answer the following questions:

What internal influences are there within your organisation?

What are the external influences?

Who are your internal and external stakeholders and what influences them?

▶ Activity 6

With reference to equality legislation, answer the following questions:

What are the nine protected characteristics?

What equality and diversity responsibilities does the employer have?

What would you consider to be appropriate behaviours to display as a team leader?

Topic consolidation

▶ Test yourself

1. The leader who holds the power and supervises their team directly is a:

   ☐ paternalistic leader
   ☐ autocratic leader
   ☐ laissez-faire leader
   ☐ democratic leader.

2. The FUEL model of coaching allows:

   ☐ the team leader to take control
   ☐ the individual to avoid actions
   ☐ the individual to come up with their own solutions
   ☐ the team leader to delegate.

3. The S in PESTLE stands for:

   ☐ strategic   ☐ selective
   ☐ social   ☐ standard

4. The P in Handy's organisational culture model stands for:

   ☐ power   ☐ paternal
   ☐ progress   ☐ positive.

5. The nine protected characteristics include:

   ☐ age, race, wealth
   ☐ religion, race, disability
   ☐ age, parenthood, maternity
   ☐ maternity, wealth, race

6. The Equality Act 2010 specifically protects employees in relation to:

   ☐ promotion   ☐ pay rises
   ☐ recruitment   ☐ holidays.

7. When planning a team member's development, I am using the following coaching model:

   ☐ GROW   ☐ FUEL
   ☐ CLEAR   ☐ BOOST

8. The kinaesthetic learning style relates to:

   ☐ seeing   ☐ doing
   ☐ hearing   ☐ reading.

9. The S in PESTLE stands for:

   ☐ smart   ☐ social
   ☐ specific   ☐ special.

2

People and team management

What is people and team management?

The people within an organisation, its employees, are its biggest asset. The performance and attitude of these individuals can result in its success or failure. It is the team leader's job to lead, motivate and train the team while maintaining discipline and evaluating performance.

A team leader needs to balance all aspects of managing a team so that they are positive and productive. There are models and theories that can be applied in the workplace that you can use with the range of people within your team.

Belbin's nine team roles

Behaviours

Inclusive – Open, approachable, authentic and able to build trust with others. Seeks views of others.

Agile – Is creative, innovative and enterprising when seeking solutions to business needs.

Professionalism – Sets an example and is fair, consistent and impartial.

Link to the standard

Knowledge Area 1: Outcome Topic 2.1

Dr Meredith Belbin created the model Belbin's nine team roles in the late 1980's, shown in table 1. The model is based on behaviours displayed within a team, their strengths, limitations and those that are seen as allowable weaknesses.

By using Belbin, team leaders can identify an individual's behavioural strengths and allowable weaknesses to create a balanced team. By extending this knowledge to the team, it enables individuals to have a greater self-understanding, leading to effective communications and collective mood that they can contribute and make a difference at work.

How could you use Belbin's model in your own team?

Belbin's nine team roles	
Plant	Implementors
Resource investigator	Completer finishers
Monitor evaluators	Team workers
Coordinators	Shapers
Specialists	

Table 1: What do each of the roles mean to you?

The nine team roles

You may not need all of the roles within your team, and you may not have nine team members. The model is designed to be flexible and it may mean that one team member displays characteristics and behaviours for more than one role. As each role will have strengths and add value to your team, there will be a counter-balance of an allowable weakness, which can be managed once you and your team are aware of it; see Table 2.

Key term

Bureaucracy – A system for controlling processes with rigid and inflexible rules.

The role	Strengths	Allowable weaknesses	How do they work best?
Plant	Has original ideas, suggestions and proposals. Happy to deal with complex problems.	Unconventional and can be preoccupied with what they are working on, becoming unaware of the rest of the team's activity.	They need time to think and perform best when they are not bound by **bureaucracy** or a very structured workplace.
Resource investigator	Has an outgoing personality, brings ideas and information to the team. Good as the team's sales person, diplomat, liaison officer or explorer.	Enthusiasm can fade as they prefer to move on to the next task. Does not always focus on the detail.	They enjoy working with colleagues and usually thrive in fast-pace teams where they can act on opportunities.
Monitor evaluator	Serious team member who tends to be logical, impartial and objective.	Can be overly critical and slow moving. May come across as boring, as they often lack the ability to inspire others.	They like a strategic situation where they can make decisions that can result in either success or failure.
Coordinators	Good at clarifying team objectives and establishing priorities.	Potential to over-delegate.	In a collaborative environment, they like to have some responsibility, autonomy and control.

Table 2: How do your team members align to these roles?

You may be able to bring a team of people together, where you can ensure each of the roles are covered, or you may be working with an existing team. When working with an existing team, you should establish the current roles within your team to find out the overall team's strengths and limitations and identify any gaps.

Certain roles may only be required for a short period, such as the specialist, who you can bring in as a consultant for a specific part of a project.

Tuckman's four stages of team development

Behaviours

Takes responsibility – Drive to achieve in all aspects of work.

Inclusive – Open, approachable, authentic and able to build trust with others. Seeks views of others.

Agile – Is creative, innovative and enterprising when seeking solutions to business needs. Positive and adaptable, responds well to feedback and need for change.

Professionalism

Key term

Cohesive – United and working together effectively.

Dr Bruce Tuckman developed his four stages of team building in 1965. In his model he identifies the link between the relationship in the group and their focus on the task to be achieved. A fifth phase was added in the 1970s, which refers to the completion of the task.

The four stages are forming, storming, norming and performing. The fifth stage is adjourning; see table 3.

Tuckman's four stages of team development	
STAGE 1 – FORMING At this stage the team do not have a shared understanding of the tasks or objectives. They have little care for each other's views or values as the roles have not been developed within the team. Team members behave independently and are likely to be on their best behaviour.	STAGE 2 – STORMING The team start to become more inward looking by becoming more concerned with other team members' values and points of view. They will also start to notice problems that other team members may have. Competition between team members will start to emerge and power struggles may start to occur.
STAGE 3 – NORMING Confidence and trust will start to be developed at this stage. The team will start to work together as a **cohesive** unit and they will begin to make commitments to each other as they start working together.	STAGE 4 – PERFORMING The team will start to work together as a fully functioning and productive team. The leadership will be decided by situations as they arise rather than company protocol. The basic principles and social aspects of the organisation's decisions are considered.
STAGE 5 – ADJOURNING This is the final stage that Tuckman added to cover the end of a project or task. It is at this stage that the team may break up as their work is complete. Teams will only reach this stage when they are fully functioning at a high level. It is often here that a restructuring may take place and new teams are formed, so that the expertise within the original team is spread across these new teams and the Tuckman cycle begins again.	

Table 3: At what stage is your team working?

The role of the team leader during the four stages

As the team transition through each of the Tuckman stages, the team leader's role will change in order to manage and shape the progress of the team's development. Table 4 explains the role of the team leader during Tuckman's four stages of team development.

Tuckman stage	Your role as team leader
Forming	At this first stage, you should provide **directive** leadership and a clear team structure. Communicate and clarify roles ensuring objectives are SMART and understood by all in the team.
Storming	Once the team have formed, you should then provide a team focus to avoid any distractions. You will also need to be directive in decision-making.
Norming	This is the stage where you will take on a participative role and be fully involved in the task or project the team are working on.
Performing	You should now monitor and review the performance of the team. Identify strengths and weaknesses as well as agree an appropriate improvement plan. Coaching and feedback are important at the stage where you will empower your team to make most of the decisions.
Adjourning	Recognise the strength and competence of your team and encourage them in any organisational restructure to enable them to continue to grow as the cycle begins again with the new teams created.

Table 4: What stage do you think you have reached?

Key term

Directive – An order or command.

Actions a team leader can take to promote effective team dynamics

1. Determine purpose and define roles within the team.

2. Clarify aims and objectives and set clear goals.

3. Give support and access to resources.

4. Promote positive working relationships and mutual respect.

5. Be proactive in giving regular feedback.

6. Acknowledge reward and success.

>>>>> **Theories and models of motivation**

Key terms

Hierarchy – A system where items are organised and ranked in order of importance, status or authority.

Deficiency – Failing or shortcoming

Link to the standard

Knowledge Area 1: Outcome Topic 2.1

Maslow's **hierarchy** of needs theory is a framework around which humanistic psychology is built. It is a belief that people have a desire to reach their maximum potential. It is a stage-based theory, where the individual needs to complete one stage before moving on to the next. However, not all people will move through all of the stages.

In order to be motivated at work, Maslow recognised that employees needs should be satisfied. Maslow organised these needs into a hierarchy of importance to the individual where the lower needs had to be satisfied before the individual moved into higher order needs.

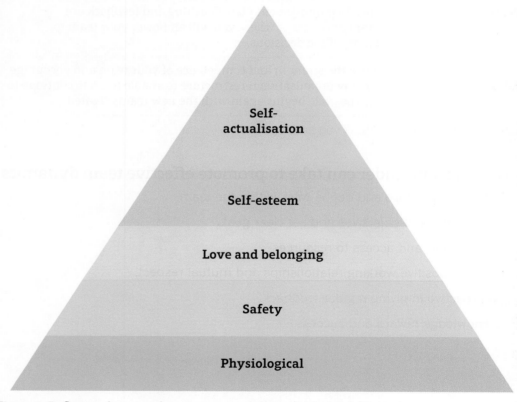

Figure 1: Reflect on how you have progressed through Maslow's hierarchy

The stages of Maslow explained

The first four stages Maslow identified as **deficiency** needs (D-needs) and the final stage as growth needs (B-needs). He recognised that individuals are motivated towards meeting the next stage of their needs and the longer the need is not met, the greater the desire to achieve that need. For example, if one of the physiological needs is not met, such as food, then the longer the need for food, the hungrier that person will become. Until that hunger is satisfied, the individual will find it difficult to think about the next stage.

People will move around the stages depending on what is going on in their life. Growth needs do not stem from a lack of something, but rather from a desire to grow as a person. The individuals work through the first four stages of needs, and once the deficit is satisfied that need will disappear, and the focus will be directed onto the next stage. In understanding Maslow's hierarchy of needs, you will be able to talk through these issues and recognise the stage each of your team member's has reached.

How is Maslow applied in the workplace?

As a team leader, you may see behaviours in your team members that are difficult to explain or understand. Through discussions with them, you may learn about issues outside of the workplace that are having an effect on their performance and behaviour. By understanding Maslow's hierarchy of needs, see table 5, you will be able to talk through these issues and recognise the stage where your team member is. This will help you to determine the help and support they may need. If their needs are not met at the physiological stage, then it is likely that your team member will not function very well. This first stage will take priority over all of the other needs and will need to be resolved in order for them to move forward.

Maslow's hierarchy of needs – what does this mean?	
Physiological	This is basic needs such as food, water, warmth, sleep and/or rest.
Safety	This could be financial security such as having a job or property. It is also physical and personal security such as family, health or stability in everyday life.
Love and belonging	This is the need for friendship, family and social interactions.
Self-esteem	Having respect and recognition from others, self-confidence, achievement and status.
Self-actualisation	At this stage, the individual can see opportunities for innovation and creativity, personal growth and fulfilment as well as learning and development.

Table 5: Are the needs of your team members being fulfilled?

Behaviours

Takes responsibility – Determination when managing difficult situations.

Inclusive – Seeks views of others.

Herzberg's two-factor theory

Herzberg's theory has close links to Maslow. He identified that job satisfaction and job dissatisfaction act independently of each other. He noted that there are factors that will influence either one or the other. He called these hygiene and motivator factors. In order to motivate your team, both must be addressed; see table 6.

Herzberg two-factor motivational theory		
Motivator	Recognition and status	Motivators are more to do with the actual job. The more interesting you can make the job for your team members, giving them responsibility, recognition and promotion, the more motivated they are likely to become. This will lead to them feeling a greater sense of achievement and more motivation.
	Opportunity for promotion	
	Greater responsibility	
	Stimulating work	
	Sense of achievement	
Hygiene Factor	Good working conditions	The hygiene factors are those which surround the job. For example, your team will expect a reasonable level of working conditions and pay. They will be happier if they have a positive relationship with their colleagues, but this alone is unlikely to make them work harder. However, if any of these hygiene factors are missing, then your team members are likely to become demotivated.
	Job security	
	Relationship with manager and colleagues	
	Wages, salaries and fringe benefits	

Table 6: Which factors need addressing in your team?

Recognition and reward as a motivational tool

Your team members are likely to be motivated by reward, which can take many forms. It is important that you use these motivational techniques appropriately so that you have the desired effect – a happy and motivated workforce.

Extrinsic rewards

These are tangible rewards that are usually linked to financial payments, such as increased salary, incentives, bonuses or other benefits. **Extrinsic** payments are externally set by a company, rather than an individual team leader. While they may start as being a great motivator, once the financial reward becomes the 'norm' to the team member, they are likely to become less motivated as they start to look for increased financial rewards that may not be available to them.

Intrinsic rewards

These are more about rewarding team members through recognition, empowerment or role development. **Intrinsic** rewards are more likely to lead to personal fulfilment as your team members feel a sense of contribution and feel they are doing meaningful work with real value.

Total reward

This is when both intrinsic and extrinsic rewards are combined to create a strategy used to attract, motivate and retain team members.

Risks involved in the use of rewards

Sometimes a reward does not engage or motivate team members. For example, if your team feel that their working conditions are poor any amount of reward may not sufficiently motivate them. Another risk when reward is used is when team members display inappropriate or unproductive activity or behaviour. For example, competitive team members may lose their sense of team-working as they focus on their own reward rather than that of the whole team. Likewise, those team members who are not achieving may become demotivated as their colleagues take all the reward. This can lead to divisions among team members.

Key terms

Extrinsic – External or coming from the outside.
Intrinsic – The essential part of something.

Behaviours

Takes responsibility – Determination when managing difficult situations.
Professionalism – Operates within organisational values.

Link to the standard

Knowledge Area 1: Outcome Topic 2.1
Skills Area 1: Outcome Topic 2.1

Summary

In this section you have learned about different models to use when building teams and managing people. This has included team dynamics and motivational techniques and how to apply them at work. This section has covered:

- Belbin's nine team roles, their strengths and allowable weaknesses
- Tuckman's four stages of team development, the behaviours likely to be displayed and your role as team leader
- Maslow's hierarchy of needs and the effect it can have on individuals if any of the needs are missing
- Herberg's two-factor theory and how job satisfaction and job dissatisfaction act independently of each other
- recognition and reward as a motivational technique.

Human resources

Link to the standard 🔗

Knowledge Area 1: Outcome Topic 2.2

Behaviours Ⓑ

Takes responsibility – Determination when managing difficult situations.

Inclusive – Seeks views of others.

Professionalism – Sets an example and is fair, consistent and impartial. Operates within organisational values.

Human resources (HR) functions

Human resources is the function or department within a business focused on activities relating to its employees. They will manage and implement specific HR functions, such as recruitment and selection of new employees and often have responsibility for staff training and development.

The HR function may oversee the management of employee relations including disputes and grievances. Part of their function is to advise managers and employees on employment laws and regulations, including workplace safety. HR will also manage performance appraisals and maintain employee personal records.

The HR department will have the latest company policies and procedures to support the running of business operations and support relations between management and employees, helping to retain and motivate the workforce.

Your HR department should always be available to you. How would you contact them?

When would you be likely to work with HR?

The relationship between the team leader role and HR

As a team leader you are likely to refer to the HR function within your organisation when you need advice and information. For example, if you have a team member who is pregnant, you might contact your HR department to find out what their maternity leave entitlement is, enabling you to plan staffing in their absence and advise them of their rights and the options available to them.

If a team member queries how much holiday they have left to take, you would check with your HR department to confirm the exact amount of days owed to them.

You are also likely to work with HR when recruiting new members of staff. Table 6 details a scenario of how the team leader might work with their HR department.

During the interview and final stages of recruiting, you are likely to liaise with the HR department to exchange relevant information and/or ask advice, such as checking on the legal requirements in employing an applicant who has only lived in the UK for six months.

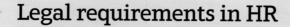

Legal requirements in HR

Working Time Regulations 1998

The purpose of the act is to govern weekly working time as well as daily and weekly rest period. It also covers employee's entitlement to paid leave. It is summarised in table 7.

Possible positive impacts	Possible negative impacts	Importance of the Working time Regulations Act 1998
Flexibility of the workforce Increase in safe working conditions as staff get sufficient rest Increase in employee motivation Good work-life balance	Increase in administration and added costs to the business Burden on small businesses Insufficient staff to cover rest periods Difficulties in managing staff holidays Can lead to failure in meeting targets and/or deadlines	The act was introduced to ensure the well-being of all employees and to ensure compliance with employment law. Having this act in place has also reduced the number of workplace accidents as staff are fully rested and do not work too many hours over long periods of time.

Table 7: Summary of Working Time Regulations 1998

Employment Rights Act 1996

This act sets out **statutory** employment rights of workers and employees. It states that all employees must have a contract of employment and sets out the law around unfair dismissal, redundancy provision, dismissal notice period, protection of wages and time off work for public duties, such as jury service, shown in table 8.

Possible positive impacts	Possible negative impacts	Importance of the Employment Rights Act 1996
Ensures that employees are treated fairly Gives increased job security Prevents or manages conflict	Increased administration with a cost to the business to implement and administer	This act protects the well-being of employees and ensures the business is compliant with employment law.

Table 8: Summary of Employment Rights Act 1996

Flexible Working Regulations 2014

This act covers employees' rights to flexible working arrangements and it is the responsibility of the employer to consider requests for flexible working. It is summarised in table 9. This could be the numbers of hours an employee works and/or when and where they work. For example, an employee may request to work in term-time only where they have a permanent contract of employment, but can take paid and unpaid holidays during school holidays. Other requests could include job-sharing, to work part-time, or agree annual hours, where hours will be worked over a year.

Possible positive impacts	Possible negative impacts	Importance of the Flexible Working Regulations Act 2014
Flexibility of the workforce Increase in employee motivation Work–life balance of the workforce Can reduce the level of stress for employees	Increased administration, which can be a burden on small businesses The need to review and/or change policies	This act ensures the well-being of employees and that the business is complying with employment law. Having this act in place can lead to a win-win situation when flexible working arrangements are adopted to meet the needs of the employee and the business. Used as a strategic tool, flexible working arrangements can improve individual and business performance as there is likely to be an increased level of engagement from the workforce.

Table 9: Summary of Flexible Working Regulations 2014

Health and Safety at Work Act 1974

This specifies the duties and responsibilities that employers have to their workforce, customers and members of the public while in the working environment. It also states that employees have their own responsibilities for keeping themselves and others safe while at work.

The impact of legal requirements

Recruitment and selection

There must be a transparent process in place that is fair and meets legislation requirements.

HR policies

These policies must comply with legal requirements, including pay, terms of employment written into a contract as well as working hours and employees' entitlements. There must also be written disciplinary and grievance procedures and mechanisms in place for informing the workforce of their legal rights and responsibilities. These are usually written out in full in the employee handbook or company intranet.

Equality and diversity

This policy should be clearly written up and made available to the whole workforce. As a team leader you will be responsible in ensuring that you and your team adhere to the policy at all times.

Health and safety policy and related procedures

The health and safety policy is likely to be displayed as a poster in an area where all of the workforce will see it, such as a kitchen or rest area. Alternatively, a health and safety leaflet must be given to all employees. As the team leader, you may be responsible for ensuring the health and safety poster is appropriately displayed or that employees have an up-to-date leaflet.

Training

Line managers will need to receive training on company policies and other important areas such as recruitment and selection, company values and ways of working.

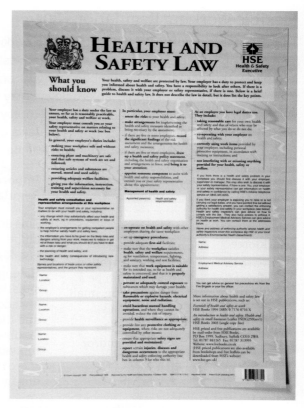

Where is the health and safety policy poster displayed in your workplace?

Summary

In this section you have learned about HR systems, their functions and legal requirements as well as their purpose and impact to an organisation. You have also learned about the importance of the HR function to the role of the team leader. This section has covered:

- human resources functions
- the relationship between the team leader role and HR
- legal requirements of the team leader/supervisor, looking at the most important government Acts and legislation
- Working Time Regulations 1998
- Employment Rights Act 1996
- Flexible Working Regulations 2014
- Health and Safety at Work Act 1974
- the impact these legal requirements have on an organisation and the team leader/supervisor role.

Performance goals and objectives

Role

The role of setting performance goals and objectives is to establish performance goals for team members, identifying any gap between current and desired performance. Once skills gaps have been identified, the next stage is to plan with the individual how the skills and/or performance will be met by setting action points and implementing the action plan. This should be monitored, so changes and improvement in performance and skills can be recorded and feedback given.

Reasons

Setting performance targets and objectives will contribute to meeting organisational aims and objectives. SMART targets/objectives should be set to establish the minimum standard requirements expected of an individual, so that outcomes can be measured and performance assessed.

Setting performance targets and objectives for individuals will also support them in knowing what their individual responsibilities are against those of the whole team and it will help them to establish their own personal **key performance indicators** (KPIs). Once established, the team members accountability is likely to be strengthened and uncertainty over standards of performance removed. This will lead to a more motivated workforce and a refinement of appropriate behaviours.

Approach

The team leader's approach to effective target setting is likely to be through negotiation with individual team members. You can work together to establish the team member's personal goals against key performance indicators. This should be followed up with regular monitoring of progress to ensure the team member is on target to meet their objectives.

Regular monitoring and discussion will also help to identify and resolve any issues that arise.

Link to the standard

Knowledge Area 1: Outcome Topic 2.3

Link to the standard

Skills Area 1 Outcome Topic 2.1

Behaviours

Inclusive – Open, approachable, authentic and able to build trust with others.

Professionalism – Open and honest. Operates within organisational values.

Key term

Key performance indicators – A set of performance measurements used in an organisation that reflects the company's values and objectives.

Goals
The desired results plans and commits to achieve the end toward which effort is establishing specific, realistic time-targeted objectives.

What are your team goals and objectives? How would you communicate these to your team?

Link to the standard

Knowledge Area 1:
Outcome Topic 2.4

Link to the standard

Skills Area 1
Outcome Topic 2.1

Measuring performance

As the team leader, you will be expected to make objective judgements on your whole team and the individual team members' performance, using relevant data and through your own observations. It is your job to communicate to your team how they are performing by recognising achievement and giving feedback on areas where they have performed well and where development is required because objectives have not been met. There are a number of feedback models that you can use. Table 10 details the BOOST model of feedback.

BOOST model	
Balanced	The feedback you give to your team member should be balanced with positive and developmental feedback. Be sure to give examples of good performance as well as examples of where improvements are required.
Observed	Base your feedback on what you have observed, especially when your feedback is around certain issues. Avoid saying what you think or feel.
Objective	Focus your feedback on the actions of your team member rather than on their personality. Keep your feedback descriptive rather than evaluative.
Specific	Give specific examples in your feedback that support your judgements on performance. Explain what it is that they have done well, or not so well.
Timely	Try to give feedback as soon as possible after the event so that you capture the actions accurately and it is still fresh in your mind and theirs.

Table 10: The BOOST model of feedback

Identification of any conflicts within the team and an analysis of your team leadership can also be established through assessing team performance. You can identify whether your own performance has led to strong, weak, efficient or inefficient leadership. For example, you notice that objectives were not met on time and you establish that you should have taken a stronger approach to hold your team to dates and sooner, to find out why.

Demonstrating appropriate behaviours by being responsible and accountable for your actions and being open and honest when providing guidance and feedback is likely to build team trust and confidence. It is important that while setting goals and objectives and monitoring progress you are consistent and impartial. You should have a positive approach and be prepared to adapt.

Techniques for measuring performance

There are a number of techniques that you can use when measuring your team's achievement of goals and objectives. The structure of your team, their location and contract status will determine which techniques are the most effective.

Progress should be reviewed against planned outputs or objectives as well as meeting targeted deadlines. Milestone reviews throughout a project or task will help to keep the individual on target. Developmental feedback can be given where necessary and interim achievements can be recognised to keep the team focused and motivated.

When reviewing the overall performance of the team you need to ask yourself questions such as; was too much or too little time allowed? Did the team meet the standard of work expected? Were there any conflicts within the team? What was the cause – could they have been avoided? Was my leadership style appropriate?

Techniques for measuring individual contribution

When reviewing individual performance, you should analyse the strengths and weaknesses of the team members, recognising individual contributions and each team member's ability to follow instructions. When targets are not being met you need to identify the reasons why. These could include a lack of the correct skills and competencies, limitation of physical resources, poor performance management, lack of communication of targets and/or standards, unmotivated team members, ineffective leadership, unrealistic targets or a lack of quality processes and procedures. The team leader's role is to be proactive to ensure that standards and performance improve, lessons are learned and feedback given with a viable action plan.

When analysing strengths and weaknesses, look at skills, communication, understanding and motivation

Identifying improvements needed

There are likely to be several areas for improvement within a team and individual performance. The main areas are outlined in Table 11.

	Techniques in identifying improvements needed
Team cohesion	Can you identify any issues in the way the team are working together? Is there a positive atmosphere and rapport between the team members? Are the team members willing to help each other?
Contributions from individuals	Are there any team members whose contribution is weak? Why are their contributions weak? How can this team member be supported?
Distribution of tasks	Have the tasks been distributed fairly across the team? Have individual workloads and skills sets been taken into consideration before allocating tasks?
Team conflicts	What are the conflicts within the team? Have they been **rationalised**? What are the likely resolutions? Are there any quick wins? Do I need to address any issues with specific team members?

Key terms

Cohesion – United and working together.
Rationalised – Attempt to explain or justify.

Link to the standard

Knowledge Area 1:
Outcome Topic 2.4
Skills Area 1:
Outcome Topic 2.1

Behaviours **B**

Takes responsibility
Inclusive
Agile
Professionalism

Link to the standard

Knowledge Area 1:
Outcome Topic 2.4

Skills Area 1:
Outcome Topic 2.2

Utilisation of individual skills	Has each team member been allocated the appropriate tasks to maximise their skills set? How could Belbin's nine team roles model be used?
Standards expected	Have the expected standards been fully communicated to the team and understood? Have training needs been identified for team members?
Team communications	Do communication channels need to be improved? If so, how can this be achieved? Did the team fully understand the objectives

Table 11: In which areas could your team improve?

Role of feedback

The way in which feedback is given is crucial to ensure that your team see your feedback as a positive experience. It should motivate them to act and feel rewarded in areas where achievements and goals have been met. Using models such as BOOST will help you to achieve this. It will also help you to ensure that your feedback highlights why performance was not as expected and explores how performance can be improved. This should lead to improving future performance and providing positive reinforcement.

Summary

In this section you have learned about the techniques you can use for measuring team performance and individual achievement of goals and objectives. You have also learned about the importance of giving feedback in a supportive manner. This section has covered:

- techniques for measuring team performance and standards
- performance goals and objectives, which must be established and any gaps then identified
- giving feedback using the BOOST model to ensure that your feedback is constructive and supports the development of the individual
- using appropriate techniques to identify improvements needed for individuals and the team.

Performance review meetings

There are several ways in which performance review meetings can be conducted.

One-to-one meetings

In these meetings the team leader will spend time with individual team members to discuss a number of topics. It is usually scheduled on a monthly basis .There may be an agenda to follow, for example in a care setting the conversation/feedback is recorded onto an official document, which is stored in the team member's personnel file. Alternatively, it may be less formal where topics are decided at the beginning of the meeting and the team leader makes brief notes of the conversation. In either case, the team leader should give the team member an opportunity to have input into the content of the meeting and an accurate record of the conversation and feedback should be provided for future reference.

How often do you have one-to-one meetings with your team?

Personal development plan (PDP)

A PDP is a formal working document where the development needs of an individual are recorded. This is likely to include objectives, which will be set and agreed between the team leader and the team member. It will also include actions needed, specific processes and deadlines in order to help the team member achieve their objectives. The team leader may discuss and draw up a PDP as part of a one-to-one meeting with the team member. This is normally reviewed and updated on a regular basis, such as quarterly. The combination of these PDPs would then contribute towards, and be the basis for, a formal appraisal meeting.

Formal appraisal meetings

Formal appraisals usually occur once or twice a year. It is a time when the team leader discusses the performance, skills, knowledge and behaviours of an individual and helps them identify their strengths and areas for development. It is an opportunity to discuss objectives met since the last appraisal, evaluate how they have been met, or not, and to set new objectives. This is also a time for discussing aspirations and career development plans.

360 degree feedback

Here, feedback is given by peers and direct reports as well as the manager. For example, the team member will give feedback to their team leader as part of the managing performance process. This enables the manager to receive feedback on how others perceive them, which they can compare to how they perceive themselves. It helps individuals to understand their own behaviours and performance from a different perspective and it increases communication between team members through peer to peer feedback. 360 degree feedback must be carefully managed to ensure that feedback is constructive and supports individuals to improve their performance, skills and behaviours and not used to demotivate or upset individuals.

Best practice in conducting performance reviews

Whichever performance review format is used, best practice should be used. Table 12 provides some examples of best practice.

Link to the standard

Knowledge Area 1:
Outcome Topic 2.5

Skills Area 1:
Outcome Topic 2.2

Behaviours

Inclusive – Open, approachable, authentic, and able to build trust with others.

Agile – Positive and adaptable, responds well to feedback and need for change.

Professionalism – Open and honest. Operates within organisational values.

Best practice in performance reviews	
Agree on performance expectations	Ensure that your team member has input and agrees to objectives or outcomes – including deadlines and action points.
Plan	Ensure you enter the performance review meeting fully prepared with discussion topics and organisational objectives that will form part of your team member's objectives. Encourage your team member to plan in advance. This could include them completing a pre-meeting self-assessment of their performance, including their strengths, weaknesses and what they want to achieve going forward. A plan should also be agreed and drawn up following the review, including actions for both the team leader and team member.
Clarify the purpose and process	As the team leader, you may already know what the objectives for individual team members should be. However, you should not 'impose' these objectives, but rather obtain the team members buy-in and agreement by clarifying the purpose and process, so that the team member is likely to come up with the same objectives.
Focus on performance and improvement	The performance review should focus on the actual performance and required improvement of the team member, as well as the purpose and intended outcomes.
Provide learning and development opportunities	The areas for improvement and/or development that have been identified should be followed up with opportunities in order to improve and progress. This may be with formal training, or through less formal methods, such as coaching and observing others, or a combination of both.
Give constructive and consistent feedback	Ensure your feedback is constructive, fair and consistent across the whole of your team. Focus on the business objectives, use humour where appropriate and maintain eye contact while giving feedback. Choose a suitable time and place, be caring and give your team member the opportunity to ask you questions on the feedback you are giving.

Table 12: Do you include these practices in your performance reviews?

Managing absence

Team members may be absent from work for a number of different reasons. It is important that as their team leader you know what these reasons are and are able to help and support them so they can return to work as soon as they are ready, or possible. Reasons for absence include sickness, family or caring responsibilities, bereavement, annual leave, jury service, etc.

Your organisation will have a process to manage planned and unplanned absence. For planned absence, such as holidays, there may be request forms that the employee completes. It is your responsibility to decide if the request can be honoured by assessing your staffing levels to maintain levels to continue operations. Alternatively, time may be owed to the individual and they are entitled to the time off.

For unplanned absence, attendance and absence policies should be reviewed and used by you and your team. These can be obtained from your HR department or found in your staff handbook. For example, the staff planned absence policy will state when and how the team member must report their absence, e.g. in person and by telephone. Individual absence records may be kept by the HR department and it could be your responsibility to advise HR of their absence. If you work for a smaller company, you may keep these records on behalf of your employer. For long-term absence, your company is likely to have a return to work policy. This may start with an interview where the absence is discussed and a plan put into place to ease the team member back into their role. If the team member is not ready to return to work, medical opinions may be necessary, such as a doctor's report.

Factors that can impact on performance

There are several factors that can impact on the performance of individuals. These are shown in Table 13.

Factors that impact on performance	
Non-work	Personal difficulties that team members may have, such as finance, family and/or relationship problems, or their lifestyle. When an individual has issues in their private life, it can affect the way that they perform at work (see Maslow's hierarchy of needs).
Individual	Personal behaviours, attributes, experiences, attitudes, resilience and ability to cope will be different amongst your team members. Some will have a better resilience to situations and ability to cope than others. Physical and mental health can also impact on an individual's performance.
Work environment	Work demands, level of control and/or support, clarity of role, working relationships and any organisational changes are all factors that can impact of an individual's performance. If a team member feels unsure of or uncomfortable in their working environment, it is likely to have a negative impact on their performance.
Work performance	Another factor to consider as a team leader is the productivity, engagement, motivation, error rate or absences of your team members.

Table 13: Which factors impact on your team members' performance?

Link to the standard

Knowledge Area 1:
Outcome Topic 2.5

Skills Area 1:
Outcome Topic 2.2

Link to the standard

Knowledge Area 1:
Outcome Topic 2.5

Skills Area 1:
Outcome Topic 2.2

Behaviours

Inclusive – Seeks views of others.

Professionalism – Operates within organisational values

Key terms

Amicably – In a friendly and peaceful manner.

Escalation – To increase the intensity or seriousness of a situation.

Tribunal – A board or panel set up to settle a dispute.

Disciplinary and grievance

Difficulties can arise in the relationship between employees and employers. These challenges can be dealt with fairly and consistently when there are organisation procedures in place that support and protect the perspectives and interests of both parties.

It is in the interest of both parties to resolve any disciplinary or grievance procedures **amicably** where possible, to avoid **escalation** to **tribunal** and so that working relationships can be re-established. Make yourself familiar with your organisation's policies and procedures and seek the support of your HR department or line manager if you have to deal with either a disciplinary issue or grievance from a team member.

Disciplinary definition:
Procedure to deal with employee misconduct or unsatisfactory performance

Grievance definition:
Framework for the quick and effective resolution of workplace issues

Why is it important to follow disciplinary or grievance process?
Ensures a reasonable standard of behaviour on both sides
Reduces the likelihood of breach of contract claims
Adherance to the processes will be considered in an employment tribunal case.

Figure 2: Identify the steps you would take in a discipline or grievance procedure

Summary

In this section you have learned about techniques you can use for managing your team's performance, including how to conduct effective reviews of their performance and provide them with constructive feedback and reward for their achievements. It has also included how grievance and disciplinary procedures can be used in correcting underperformance using performance management techniques. This section has covered:

- different types of performance review meetings such as one-to-one meetings, PDP meetings, appraisal meetings, etc. and how they are likely to be conducted
- best practice in conducting performance reviews
- how to manage absence of team members, understanding the reasons behind their absence and the action you can take
- disciplinary and grievance, what they are and procedures to follow

Activities

▶ **Activity 1**

a. Using examples from your workplace, produce a written account on the theories and models of team building, including how you can develop a high performing team.

b. Write a reflective account that considers:

   a. how you and your team communicate

   b. how effective you and your team are when communicating with others

   c. what improvements you could make in the future.

▶ **Activity 2**

a. Locate the policies within your organisation relating to the HR function and give an example of how each policy is implemented in your workplace.

b. Identify the person to contact in the event of needing support with your HR systems and explain the extent to which they can support you.

▶ **Activity 3**

a. Explain why you would make individuals aware of issues with their performance and what measures you would take to ensure that the situation is handled sensitively.

b. What organisational processes would you use to agree a course of action to address underperformance?

c. Collate evidence that you have:

   a. undertaken a review with individuals within your team

   b. agreed SMART objectives for each team member, that relate to your organisational goals and/or strategy

   c. undertaken follow-up reviews with each team member.

▶ **Activity 4**

a. Using examples from your own workplace, explain the use of performance measures.

b. Using your organisational performance measures, give examples of how these performance measures have been reviewed against two of your team members, identifying their achievements and areas for development.

▶ **Activity 5**

a. Identify the appraisal process within your organisation and use it with two of your team members.

b. Explain the discipline and grievance procedures within your own organisation and how these procedures provide ways to address discipline, grievance and underperformance.

Topic consolidation

▶ Test yourself

Use these questions to help you reflect on your understanding and experience and identify areas you need to develop.

1. Belbin's nine team roles

   ☐ I can find a role for each of my team members.
   ☐ I can identify more than one role for each of my team members.
   ☐ I find it difficult to identify any roles that fit with my team.
   ☐ I see a way to develop my team to make use of Belbin's nine team roles.

2. Tuckman's four stages of team development

   ☐ I can see exactly which stage my team are at.
   ☐ I would be able to explain Tuckman to my team.
   ☐ I am already familiar with Tuckman and use it all the time.
   ☐ I need to re-visit the section on Tuckman in order to apply it.

3. HR systems and functions

   ☐ I know who to contact in our HR department.
   ☐ I need to find out how I can contact our HR department.
   ☐ We do not have an HR department, but I know who to contact if I have any questions or queries.
   ☐ We do not have an HR department and I need to find out what to do if I have any questions or queries.

4. Legislation

   ☐ I know and understand the legal requirements in my role as a team leader.
   ☐ I can locate the Health and Safety at Work Act poster.
   ☐ I know what the nine protected characteristics are.
   ☐ I know my organisation's policies and procedures relating to legislation.

5. Measuring performance

   ☐ I review my team's performance regularly.
   ☐ I address poor performance with individual team members.
   ☐ I have a development plan in place for each of my team.
   ☐ I give regular feedback to each member of my team.

6. Managing performance

   ☐ I know what my company procedures are for managing performance.
   ☐ I follow and can demonstrate best practice in managing performance.
   ☐ I know what to do when any of my team are absent.
   ☐ I understand the difference between disciplinary and grievance.

7. In Maslow's hierarchy of needs, having respect and recognition from others will help to meet the following need:

   ☐ safety
   ☐ self-esteem
   ☐ love and belonging
   ☐ self-actualisation

3

The project life cycle

Building good relationships is the key to the success of any organisation. The organisation needs to build trust with all its key stakeholders to ensure that they can work together to help them achieve the objectives.

In this section you will find out that as a team leader or supervisor, you play an important role in building and maintaining relationships with the different groups of people in the organisation. You should work hard to build a positive working relationship with your team to help you work together on a day to day basis. You will learn about:

- emotional intelligence and the skills required for its effective use
- negotiation and management of conflict, causes of conflict, techniques to manage it and possible consequences
- how you facilitate cross team relationships.

Emotional intelligence

Key terms

Emotional intelligence
– Is the capacity to be
aware of, control and
express one's emotions.

**Interpersonal
relationships** –
Connections or
interactions that are
developed between two
or more people who share
common goals in the
workplace.

Empathy – The ability
to share and understand
other people's feelings.

Behaviours

Inclusive – Open,
approachable, authentic
and able to build trust
with others.

Link to the standard

Knowledge Area 1:
Outcome Topic 3.1

Skills area

Knowledge Area 1:
Outcome Topic 3.1

Being aware of your own emotions is an important skill in building relationships with others at work. You have to consider **emotional intelligence** when working with your team and other people, both inside and outside the organisation.

Emotional intelligence is about being aware of your own emotions and knowing how to control them. Ensuring that you make decisions and act without being driven by your emotions is vital, so that the actions you take are the right ones.

You may on occasions feel upset or frustrated at work. Knowing how to control these emotions when interacting with others is key in maintaining and building relationships. You should learn how to express your emotions without causing upset or conflict with others and how to conduct **interpersonal relationships** with good judgement and **empathy**. Understanding and sharing other people's emotions will help you to work effectively as a team leader or supervisor.

Do you consider how your actions make others feel?

Using emotional intelligence effectively in the workplace

There are a number of factors to consider when using emotional intelligence effectively in your role as team leader or supervisor.

Using empathy to calm conflict situations

Understanding the emotions of others and knowing how they feel can help you when dealing with challenging situations. If you can consider the viewpoint of the other person and how they feel, you can find a way to defuse the situation and move on. Think about how you would feel if you were them and use this perspective to consider what you should do.

De-escalating conflict

Sometimes, conflict arises rapidly, and you may be unsure of the trigger. Under pressure we make decisions about what to do and say very quickly. Slow down and think about your own actions. This will give you time to consider all options and make a conscious decision about the best course of action. Giving each other time will de-escalate the conflict. In conflict situations arising within your team, ask people to step away from the discussion and return to it once everyone has taken time to reflect.

Minimising your own negative emotional reactions

As a team leader or supervisor, you are in a position of responsibility and you need to act as a good role model. Think about your own reactions and minimise your own negative emotions. You should avoid acting on emotions, putting them aside and act only on the information and facts available. As a representative of your organisation any negative emotional reaction from you could reflect badly on the organisation and could make the situation worse.

Controlling your own emotions in tense situations

You may feel uncomfortable with conflict or in tense situations. You may want to avoid the situation, make an off-hand comment or even laugh. Witnessing other people's negative emotions or conflicts is difficult. Think carefully about how your emotions and reaction will make other people feel. Remaining calm and considering people's feelings will help you to control your emotions and manage the conflict.

Demonstrating sensitivity to others' feelings

In conflict situations, make sure that you demonstrate your sensitivity to other people's feelings and act to reassure them. However, this needs to be done sincerely and the other person needs to feel that you genuinely understand their feelings. Simply saying *"I understand how you feel"* may not be enough to convince them that you actually do. Confirm how they are feeling before you act.

Key term

Personal skills – Skills that help you understand yourself and develop good self-awareness.

Behaviours

Inclusive – Open, approachable, authentic, and able to build trust with others. Seeks views of others.

Link to the standard

Knowledge Area 1: Outcome Topic 3.1

Skills area

Knowledge Area 1: Outcome Topic 3.1

Personal skills

There are a number of **personal skills** that are important for you to develop in your role as team leader or supervisor.

Self-awareness

Self-awareness is the skill of understanding yourself; your strengths and limitations. You need to practise putting yourself into other people's shoes and think about how they would judge you and your behaviour. Knowing how other people consider your actions is essential if you are to adapt your behaviour in future. This will create effective work relationships with your team.

Emotional awareness

This is the ability to read your own and others' emotions. Considering others' and your own emotions will enable you to develop and improve your interaction with them. For example, a colleague might feel stressed and overwhelmed in their role. By adapting your tone of voice and body language to help alleviate their stress, you can increase the chance of your message being understood.

Accurate self-awareness

Be realistic and honest about yourself so that the person you are is portrayed accurately. By not being fully self-aware you could take on too much work, find a task overwhelming, difficult or even cause conflict with others. It is useful to talk to others to find out how you are perceived. This will help you develop accurate self-awareness.

Self-confidence

Believing in your own ability and worth will help you make the correct decisions and have confidence in them being successful. Self-confidence can also develop other people's confidence in your ability to do your job. This can help your team to trust you and help avoid conflict. However, self-confidence can sometimes be viewed as over-confidence or even arrogance, which can cause conflict and ineffective working relationships.

Self-regulation

In your role as a team leader or supervisor, self-regulation involves a number of essential skills as shown in table 1.

Self-control	You should learn to control your own actions, behaviours and body language. Even when under pressure and in challenging circumstances, you must demonstrate self-control to ensure that the situation is resolved effectively.
Trustworthiness	As a team leader or supervisor, you are trusted to be honest and truthful. Your team, customers and wider organisation need to trust you to do your job and keep details of your work and team confidential.
Conscientiousness	Being conscientious involves taking the obligations of your role seriously and working hard to ensure that you achieve your goals. You should drive the projects you are involved in to ensure that they are completed. On a daily basis, you will also ensure that your team deliver all the tasks and activities they are allocated.
Adaptability	As a team leader or supervisor, you should be able to adapt to different circumstances. You may need to change your approach to managing your team or adapt your plans and strategy to meet the needs of the new situation.

Table 1: Essential skills involved in self-regulation

Motivation

Motivation is an important skill when building relationships with your team and others in the organisation as shown in table 2 .

Achievement	Striving to achieve a goal can motivate you and your team to work together on a project or task. The combined effort and sense of achievement once a goal is reached can help bond the team and build relationships.
Drive	As the main motivator in your team you should find out what drives you in your role. Drive refers to your internal motivation to fulfilling your role as a team leader or supervisor.
Commitment	As a team leader or supervisor, you should remain committed to the organisation and your role. This commitment will help you motivate others and help you develop the team's relationship.
Initiative	At times you may need to think of new ideas and ways of doing things. Your ability to use your initiative can help you to be successful in your role and motivate your team.
Optimism	Sometimes things can go wrong and your team may feel despondent. You should remain optimistic about the task, displaying confidence and a belief to the team that you can be successful. This will help motivate them and develop a strong working relationship.

Table 2: Aspects of motivation

Social skills

You should ensure that you are empathetic when working with others to help develop and maintain good working relationships. Empathy is:

- seeing things from others' points of view by imagining what people are thinking and feeling

- understanding others by getting to know the people you are working with

- matching others' emotions and using emotional intelligence to demonstrate you understand

- validating others' perspectives by acknowledging them as important which can be achieved by listening and responding.

These skills all contribute to building positive relationships at work

Social skills are one of the most important sets of skills in building effective relationships. These are the skills used to interact with others and include verbal and non-verbal communication (see Section 4.1). Examples of social skills are outlined below.

- Influencing to affect people's opinions or actions. You will have influence over the views and actions of your team and can use this to help achieve the organisation's objectives. However, you should not use this influence to pressure your team to do what you want them to do.

- Communicating well is vital to working effectively as a team leader or supervisor and without good communication skills you will find it difficult to build good working relationships.

- Conflict management is the skill of identifying possible conflicts and developing strategies to avoid them. This is a really important skill in your role, as sometimes conflicts will threaten to damage relationships in your team.

- **Leadership** is the skill of leading and motivating a team.

- A change catalyst works to drive and guide the organisation through periods of change and uncertainty to achieve the end goal.

- You should build bonds with, and between, members of your team. This will help ensure that you have a shared goal and can work together towards their successful completion.

- **Collaboration** is agreeing and working towards a shared goal. Sharing and agreeing the objectives of the organisation, task or project will help you work well with others.

- **Cooperating** and working together as a team will help you develop a good working relationship with the rest of your team.

You will also need to review and evaluate the team capabilities. By looking at the range of skills, qualities and experience of individuals, you will ensure that overall you have everything needed to work effectively as a team. This includes looking at the different personalities involved and selecting a balance of different types of people and managing their relationships.

Key terms

Leadership – The act of leading and motivating for a common goal.
Collaboration – Working together to achieve a shared goal.
Cooperation – Two or more people working together.

Behaviours

Takes responsibility – Drive to achieve in all aspects of work.

Link to the standard

Knowledge Area 1: Outcome Topic 3.1

Skills area

Knowledge Area 1: Outcome Topic 3.1

Summary

This section has been about understanding emotional intelligence and its importance in building effective relationships at work.
- The personal skills that are important in becoming an effective team leader and creating effective teams.
- The social skills required at work to ensure that teams work effectively.

Negotiation

Negotiation strategies

You should develop a range of **negotiation** strategies to help you to build relationships with your team and others in the organisation. There are a number of different strategies you can use; see figure 1.

Figure 1: How have you used these strategies in your role?

Problem-solving

Problem-solving involves trying to find solutions to complex or difficult issues. Figure 2 shows the problem-solving cycle. The first step is to identify the problems and define all the issues involved. Once this has been done, you can then explore the possible solutions to the problem. By analysing the positive and negatives of each possible solution you can decide the best approach to take.

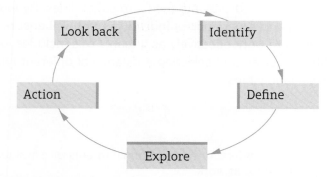

Figure 2: Use the cycle of problem-solving with an issue you are currently dealing with.

The next stage is to put the solution into action. Once it has been completed you can reflect on its successes and limitations. You may need to repeat the process if the problem has not been solved.

Contending

Contending is asserting a point of view or argument. This can cause problems, as others may feel that you are overly forceful. If this is the case it may detract from the argument you are trying to put forward. However, during a negotiation, it may be necessary to contend your point of view. This may happen if the discussion has lost focus or you feel strongly that it is moving in the wrong direction.

As a team leader or supervisor, you should assert your authority and ensure that your point of view is heard. Be aware of the method of communication and body language you use, so that you are not perceived as aggressive.

Yielding

At times in a negotiation it may be necessary to yield. You may need to accept someone else's ideas and discount your own. This may be appropriate if you realise that, on reflection, the points of view of others are better, or more suited to the situation than your own.

You may find that it is better to yield on minor issues in a negotiation, to gain the trust of your team. This may make them willing to accept your ideas on more important issues. Consider everyone's point of view and decide what is most important – winning in the negotiation or building positive relationships for the future?

Compromising

Compromising involves both sides making concessions to each other. This is a useful strategy in negotiation as all those involved feel as if they have won something. You should work with everyone involved to find the middle ground so that a compromise can be found. Encouraging everyone involved to use their emotional intelligence will help you find the compromise.

Inaction

This negotiation strategy involves letting others put forward all their points of view. This has the advantage of allowing you to consider all the information provided. It also allows others time to reflect and come to you with a compromise. However, it could say to others in the group that you are unwilling to participate. Remember that different strategies are appropriate in different situations and at different times in negotiations.

Components of a negotiation strategy

Once you have decided on your negotiation strategy, you need to be aware of the different components involved in the process; see figure 3.

Stages in the negotiation process

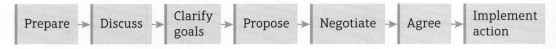

Figure 3: Implement this process in your next negotiation

- **Prepare** what you want to say and what needs to be discussed before you start the negotiation.

- **Discuss** the issues at hand and all the information available.

- **Clarify goals** so everyone is aware of what needs to be achieved.

- **Propose** the solution or strategy, giving reasons for the choice of this method. If this is in a formal meeting environment, it may be appropriate for this to be done by the chair of the meeting.

- **Negotiate** with each person explaining their views and listening to each other respectfully.

- **Agree** the strategy and outcome.

- **Implement action** once you have everyone's agreement.

Approaches in the negotiation process

You will also need to agree an approach to the negotiation process. You have a number of approaches to select from as shown in table 3.

Hard	Soft	Assertive	Empathetic
Tough, aggressive bargaining	Gentle bargaining	Strong bargaining, taking the lead	Bargaining considers emotions and views of others
Involves contending others' views or inaction	Often involves yielding to others	Often involves contending	Often involves compromising
Winning is the goal	Agreement is the goal	May result in no outcome or withdrawal	Compromise is the goal

Table 3: Approaches to negotiation

Desired negotiation outcomes

You will also need to consider what the desired outcomes may be.

- **Defeat the other party** This outcome is focused only on winning.

- **Collaborate** The different parties agree on a compromise.

- **Accommodate** Give in and agree to the strategies or outcomes proposed by others.

- **Withdraw** The negotiation is stopped and no outcome is agreed.

Finally, you should consider what is required during a negotiation.

1. You should reach an understanding. This involves understanding each others' points of view and sharing all the information available.

2. Where points of difference arise, these should be resolved so that an agreement can be made.

3. You may want to gain the advantage, by pushing forward your point of view and achieve your chosen strategy or outcome.

4. The most satisfactory outcome would be one that satisfies all interests. It may take effort and crafting to ensure that this happens.

Link to the standard

Knowledge Area 1:
Outcome Topic 3.2

Skills area

Knowledge Area 1:
Outcome Topic 3.1

What do you have to negotiate as team leader/ supervisor?

Negotiation techniques

There are a number of techniques involved at different stages in a negotiation.

Pre-negotiation

Before you start the negotiation, you should prepare and undertake a problem analysis.

Problem analysis	Analyse every aspect and detail of the problem. Explore all the issues involved. Consider all the possible solutions to the issues involved.
Preparation	Identify negotiation goals and outcomes. Conduct research on other parties. Set negotiation parameters and fall-back position. Confirm available resources.

During negotiation

What we say and do, and how these words or actions are perceived by others has a significant influence on the outcome of a negotiation.

Active listening	Demonstrate that you are engaged in the negotiations by actively listening.
Emotional control	Be aware of your own and others' emotions.
Verbal communication	Consider the words you use and how you say them.
State desired outcomes	Ensure that the desired outcomes of the negotiations are made clear and everyone is aware of them.
Questioning	Being polite but asking direct, specific questions will help you gather the information you require.
Exercising silence	It can be useful to exercise silence at some points to apply pressure on others to agree to your strategies or outcomes.
Collaboration and teamwork	Work towards agreed goals with others in the negotiation.
Problem-solving	Focus on problem-solving to ensure that the negotiation is effective in achieving its goal.
Decision-making	Analyse the positives and negatives of the options available and make a well-reasoned decision based on the evidence.
Interpersonal skills	These skills involve helping you work, interact and communicate.
Ethics and reliability	Make sure that everyone can be trusted and ethical to ensure that they treat everyone fairly.

Consequences of negotiation

There are three conclusions in a negotiation.

1. **Win** – you are able to secure all the aspects of the negotiation that you set out to achieve.

2. **Lose** – you are unable to secure the aspects of the negotiation that you set out to achieve

3. **Create alternative solutions** – all negotiating parties agree to proceed with alternative solutions that were not part of the initial negotiation.

What techniques can help you negotiate a desired outcome?

Conflict

Behaviours

Takes responsibility
– Determination when managing difficult situations.

Link to the standard

Knowledge Area 1: Outcome Topic 3.2

Skills area

Knowledge Area 1: Outcome Topic 3.1

Key terms

Conflict – A serious argument or disagreement.

Productivity – The measure of the productive output of an individual, team, machine or period of time.

At times you will encounter **conflicts** which, if not resolved, could damage the relationships in your team and ultimately their overall performance. You should work to resolve these conflicts for the good of your team and the organisation.

There are four different types of conflict you will need to be aware of.

Conflict situations	These are situations where conflicts arise in the workplace.
Substantive conflict	This is conflict around performance or the completion of tasks.
Affective conflict	This is conflict due to personal likes or dislikes of other people.
Procedural conflict	This is conflict over how to achieve a goal or resolve a problem.

Potential consequences of conflict

There are a number of consequences of conflict that can affect the whole organisation.

Impact on morale

When there is conflict in an organisation, it can impact on how people feel about their job and their motivation. This can affect the level of morale in the team.

Decreased productivity

If there is disagreement about how to complete a task, or people don't work well together, there may be a fall in the amount of work done. This means that **productivity** may decrease.

Stress and anxiety of staff

Working in an environment where there is conflict can make the people involved and/or others stressed and anxious. They may feel worried about coming to work and in the long-term they may decide to leave the organisation.

Increase in absenteeism

If people don't feel happy coming to work due to the fear of conflict, they may not turn up to work, choosing to take sick days rather than face conflict situations.

Increase in grievances

A grievance is a complaint made by one employee about another. If there is conflict at work, you may find there is an increase in the number of grievances. Each grievance will have to be investigated and this will take time, which may be lost from other activities you need to complete.

Be aware how conflict can impact your team

Increased employee turnover

If a situation escalates and becomes serious, people may leave, causing the organisation to be short-staffed and resulting in costly and time consuming recruitment and training.

Damaged organisation reputation

Ultimately, conflicts in the workplace will reflect upon and damage the organisation's reputation. Staff who leave may tell others about their experience and this may make recruiting new staff more difficult. Furthermore, if customers observe conflict, they may be reluctant to use the organisation again.

Bell and Hart's eight causes of conflict

Bell and Hart identified eight causes of conflict that you can use to identify reasons for conflict and ways to help you to avoid it in future.

- **Conflicting resources** Often in an organisation, people have to share resources and this can cause conflict. If there are not enough resources, people become frustrated and take this out on one another. Additionally, some individuals do not return resources to the correct place or damage them in some way.

- **Conflicting work style** This is all about people's different personalities in the workplace and how they sometimes may clash. In the work environment, members of staff can sometimes irritate and annoy other people, causing conflict.

Key term

Employee turnover –
The number of employees leaving the organisation.

Behaviours

Agile – Flexible to the needs of the organisation. Is creative, innovative and enterprising when seeking solutions to business needs.

Link to the standard

Knowledge Area 1: Outcome Topic 3.2

Skills area **S**

Knowledge Area 1: Outcome Topic 3.1

How would you manage a clash of personalities and work style in your team?

- **Conflicting perceptions** Perceptions are views of people, events and situations. One person can perceive an event in one way but another can see it another way: this can cause conflict as there could be disagreement about who is right.

- **Conflicting goals** Though it is important to agree and share goals in an organisation, this is not always the case. Sometimes different people in the team can have different goals and this can cause conflict.

- **Conflicting behaviour** As individuals we all act and behave differently but can frustrate and irritate other people without intent. The behaviour of others may be different to your own and can also contribute to conflict.

- **Conflicting roles** From time to time in organisations, individual roles, their responsibilities and tasks may conflict with each other. One individual may, for example, be tasked with cutting costs but another may be involved in promoting projects involving high levels of expenditure.

- **Different personal values** Each individual with have a different set of personal values. These are the factors in life they believe in and see as important. As we are all individuals, it is therefore likely that, at times, we will hold different values and beliefs that may affect how the organisation functions and how they behave.

- **Unpredictable policies** Policies and procedures change all the time in organisations and not everyone will be aware of these changes. These changes can make people feel unsettled and can cause conflict. Some people might not agree with the new policies or others might still work to different outdated policies.

Non-compliance with rules and policies

Non-compliance is the failure or refusal to follow the policies and procedures in place within an organisation, or undertake actions that disregard the best interests of the organisation. As a team leader or supervisor, you should be aware of what this involves and how to report this to the appropriate department.

Personal non-compliance or disregard for company by colleagues is shown when people don't behave or act as they should. All of the following aspects of non-compliance have the potential to cause conflict which could damage working relationships if not handled effectively.

Discriminatory behaviour

It is considered **discriminatory behaviour** when one person takes actions against another based on their personal characteristics, such as gender, race, sexual orientation, etc. This is unacceptable and should not happen in the workplace. There are laws in place to protect against discrimination at work and you will need to be aware of the requirements to ensure that this does not happen or is correctly reported in the unfortunate event that it does.

Unacceptable language

When at work, we need to think carefully about the language we use. What is acceptable at home or when talking to friends may not be acceptable in a professional environment. Swear words should never be used; they may cause offence and are unprofessional. Using certain slang words or phrases should also be avoided, as others may not understand it or find it offensive. Repeated use of unacceptable language at work could result in disciplinary action.

As the team leader or supervisor, you must set a good example. You should also ensure that you address any use of unacceptable language within your team and explain why it is not appropriate or acceptable.

Poor attendance

It is important you are aware of any member of your team who is developing a poor attendance record. There will be a section in the company staff handbook or in a policy that outlines what is expected regarding attendance. If you notice that this is becoming an issue with a member of your team, you should identify this and the reasons for it and discuss this with them, making them aware of the consequences if attendance does not improve. Make sure, while doing so, that you follow the company's policy.

Time keeping

Good time keeping is crucial in helping an organisation function and therefore you will need to monitor this with your team. They should know that they need to arrive on time and ready to work and return from breaks promptly.

Key term

Discriminatory behaviour – The actions or behaviours that discriminate unfairly based on race, gender, etc.

If someone is repeatedly late for work, try to find out why and how you can help them be prompt.

Misunderstandings

Poor communication leads to misunderstandings. In Section 4.1 you learn how to ensure that communication is effective. It is important that messages are communicated effectively. If not, the wrong message may be received or not fully understood. This could lead to wrong decisions or actions, causing conflict between team members.

Sometimes the way we communicate can cause offence or upset other people as we haven't thought carefully enough about how we communicate, the method and language used and our body language. Use the information provided in Section 4.1 to help you to encourage good communication within your team.

Competition/rivalry

Sometimes competition instead of collaboration in a team results in anti-productive behaviour. Rather than focusing on what is best for the organisation and getting the job done, team members focus more on competing with each other and winning. Competition and rivalry can be healthy; it encourages staff to work harder and provide a better quality of service. However, it can mean that conflict can arise and harms not only the team's relationships with one another but also the productivity of the organisation.

As a team leader or supervisor, you will need to be aware of each of these potential consequences or causes of conflict and identify ways to avoid them. In the next section, we will look at techniques you can use to help avoid them.

Techniques to manage conflict

There are a number of techniques you can try to help you manage conflict in the workplace.

Non-intervention

When there is conflict in the team, it may be best to leave those involved to manage the conflict themselves. Frequently, you will find that minor situations of conflict can be resolved quickly within the team with no need for intervention. The conflict may also just run its course and by intervening, you may raise the profile of the conflict and make it worse. Others may also view your involvement as unnecessary and resent your input. Therefore, wait a little while before doing anything and watch to see if the conflict can be solved within the team.

Intervention

At times it will be obvious that a conflict is serious or cannot be solved by the team alone. In these situations, acting quickly to resolve the conflict before it escalates and affects other people in the organisation is vital. You may need to protect some employees, while removing those who are most disruptive.

Be careful to make sure you know the facts before apportioning blame or responsibility to an individual. It may be best just to allow time to calm down while you gather the facts. You should help those involved reach a resolution and follow up the incident to check that there is no further conflict.

Facilitation

Depending on the nature and severity of the conflict, you may be able to facilitate those involved to find their own resolution. You could hold one-to-one or group discussions to establish the facts and give the people involved the opportunity to air their grievances and explain their point of view. This may help them to clarify their own, and other people's, positions and come to a satisfactory resolution. As the team leader or supervisor, you should manage these discussions or meetings, ensuring that they keep to the point and do not lose focus.

Behaviours

Inclusive – Open, approachable, authentic and able to build trust with others.

Link to the standard

Knowledge Area 1: Outcome Topic 3.2

Skills area

Knowledge Area 1: Outcome Topic 3.1

How would you intervene in a conflict within your team?

Use of official processes

It is paramount that you check and understand the company's policies and procedures documents to ensure that you follow official process. This is important as you need to make sure that there is no opportunity for complaints or grievances in future and you follow the rules. There may also be laws in place that need to be upheld. If you are in any doubt about an official process you should follow, check with your manager or another member of staff, so you are sure that you are doing things correctly.

Negotiation

In Section 3.2 we looked at negotiation strategies and techniques. You could use these to help you resolve a conflict within your team. This will help you seek and agree a solution with team members and work towards gaining concessions from everyone involved to reach a resolution.

When deciding which technique to use when dealing with the conflict, you should consider how serious it is. It can be useful to rank them into three groups, using a traffic light system as shown below.

Type of conflict	Suggested technique	Severity
Serious conflict	Intervention, use of official procedures	
Manageable conflict	Negotiation, facilitation	
Trivial conflict	Non-intervention, facilitation	

Consider how you use personal skills to help you find a resolution. You need to ensure that you act professionally, ensuring that you represent the values and image of the organisation at all times. Think about the cycle of problem-solving and how you could use it to help resolve the conflict. You should also consider the method of communication and ensure that it is effective.

There may be a need for mediation. This is where you work with the different people involved, getting them to talk the issues through and reach an agreement together. You will also consider how to give feedback to the people involved, so you convey the points you want to make, without causing upset and escalating the issue further.

Summary

This section has been about negotiation strategies and techniques and how to use them in the workplace.
- The different causes of conflict in teams and the potential consequences of conflict at work.
- The different techniques that can be used to manage conflict and the skills required when resolving conflict.

Facilitating cross team relationships

At times, you and your team will need to work with other teams and departments within the organisation. This will mean that as the team leader or supervisor, you will need to facilitate cross team relationships. This involves establishing and maintaining positive and effective relationships with other team leaders or supervisors and ensuring that the rest of the teams also create good working relationships. You will therefore need a good understanding of the roles and responsibilities of everyone in each of the teams and demonstrate empathy and understanding of other points of view.

Collaboration

Collaboration is a cooperative arrangement in which two or more parties work together towards a common goal. When working with other teams, you should ensure that you agree a common goal in advance and foster good working relationships to help this.

There are a number of ways to do this.

- **Brainstorming** involves everyone in the group coming up with as many ideas as they can. They will be listed and then discussed to decide which are the best ideas.

- **Affinity sorting/affinity diagrams** is a method businesses use to organise and sort information and data. When using affinity sorting/affinity diagrams the team write down their different ideas, on cards, or sticky notes. These are displayed on a table, whiteboard or wall and discussed, then ranked in order of preference and then the final idea or ideas are selected.

- **Ranking** involves taking a number of different options/alternatives and placing them in order of preference, importance or usefulness. This helps to consider all the options involved and to compare them.

Behaviours B

Agile – Is creative, innovative and enterprising when seeking solutions to business needs.

Link to the standard

Knowledge Area 3: Outcome 9

Skills area S

Building trust with and across the team, using effective negotiation and influencing skills, and managing any conflicts.

How can you improve your team's collaboration with others?

Need for collaboration

The need for collaboration may arise for a number of different reasons and it is important you understand how best to facilitate this.

Cross-disciplinary skills and insight

On occasion you might be working on a project that requires a range of different skills that are not available in your team. You may need to work with people from another department to make use of these skills. Also, people from other departments and areas of the business may have a different insight into the organisation and this may be useful at times. For example, the customer service team might have more of an insight into the needs of your customers than your team and this could help you ensure that you deliver to customer expectations.

Innovation

Working with people from other departments can help to create more new ideas and ways of doing things. Therefore cross team working can be really useful in **innovation**.

Builds trust

When different departments or areas of the business work separately, there may be some mistrust or competition between them. Working in cross team groups can break down some of the concerns and misconceptions about each other and build trust.

Communication

Very often in larger organisations, communication across departments is done remotely through emails or video calls. This can mean that communication is not always effective. If all teams are separate from one another, then communication can break down and important messages may not be shared. This could result in duplication of work or disparity of objectives.

Stakeholder/team buy-in

At times certain areas can feel disengaged and not involved in the daily running of the business. Departments may feel isolated from one another. Therefore, cross team working can be a valuable way of making sure that all stakeholders feel involved and buy in to the organisation's goals. This way everyone is working towards a shared goal and is more likely to be successful.

Greater productivity

If teams work together and become more effective, saving time and resources, the productivity of the organisation will improve. This can only be good for the organisation, as greater productivity can lead to greater profitability.

Key term

Innovation – Is the process of developing new ideas, methods and processes.

Features of effective collaboration

There are number of features of effective collaboration that you need to be aware of.

- **Shared goals** For collaboration to be effective, the whole team need to have a shared goal that they have agreed. This means that they will be working in the same direction to make the project, activity or task is successful.

- **Respect for all perspectives** Respecting everyone's point of view and having empathy for others is another feature of effective collaboration. Everyone needs to feel they can offer their contributions safely and without criticism.

- **Empowerment of individuals** For collaboration to be effective, individuals need to feel that they have the power to make decisions and act. They need to know that they can decide on the best thing to do and not always seek permission from others.

- **Open communication** Being able to communicate openly, without complaint and criticism and being able to talk to all of the other members of the team, will help make collaboration more effective. Everyone needs to have a voice to ensure that all are engaged and work to the same common goal.

- **Equal access to information** Information needs to be provided to everyone regularly, so that people can make decisions in the best interest of the team and goal. Regular updates on task allocation should ensure there is no duplication or contradiction of tasks.

- **A collective mindset** A mindset is a person's opinion or way of thinking. A collective mindset – one shared by everyone – ensures that collaboration is effective. This means that people need to work together closely to make sure they all have the same point of view. Of course, there may be disagreement and negotiation techniques may be required to develop a collective mindset.

Key term

Empowerment – Giving power and control to individuals to make decisions and act themselves.

Potential implications of ineffective collaboration

There are potential implications of ineffective collaboration which you need to understand. In your role as team leader or supervisor, you may need to take remedial action to limit these implications.

Conflict between individuals and departments

If collaboration is ineffective, it could cause conflict between individuals in the teams or between different departments. This can be really damaging as the organisation overall has shared goals and everyone needs to be working towards them. This may get in the way of organisational objectives being achieved.

Wasted resources

If information is not shared about progress and any work completed is not shared effectively, then it may result in resources being wasted. Too many resources may be used or used in the wrong place resulting in unnecessary expenditure.

Organisation's competitive ability is weakened

If collaboration is ineffective and the quality of service or products affected, then the organisation may lose customers. These customers may choose to go to the organisation's competitors and its competitive ability becomes weakened. Likewise, if resources are wasted, and costs are unnecessarily high then the organisation may have to increase pricing and lose out to its competitors.

Delays

If ineffective collaboration causes conflict or mistakes, this can slow down the processes and cause delays. This may have a knock-on effect on customers or other departments, potentially affecting the organisation's profits and reputation.

Inefficiencies

Not working effectively and spending time sorting out mistakes or negotiating to resolve conflicts may result in inefficiencies. This means that there is an increase in waste or productivity falls. Either way, this will cost the organisation money and result in less profit.

Poor lines of communication

Communication can degenerate if people do not work together effectively. The wrong message may be given or people may not be kept informed with all the information they need.

Identify the individuals and departments you collaborate with and consider how these interactions can be improved.

Managing knowledge when collaborating with other departments

The management of knowledge is crucial when working with other departments. You will need to consider how you identify and capture the organisation's intellectual assets, which are ideas, innovation and knowledge of its staff, generated when working for them.

You should identify who owns these intellectual assets and therefore who, if and when they can be shared with.

You should consider how and when to share information with others in the organisation. This is increasingly important given changes in the law, with the introduction of the General Data Protection Regulations (GDPR), which regulates how organisations store, use and pass on information.

Factors to consider

When developing cross team relationships, you will need to consider the following:

Tacit and explicit knowledge to be managed

There are two types of knowledge to be managed.

- **Tacit knowledge** is knowledge which is developed through the completion of jobs and tasks. Consider what tacit knowledge you have developed but also that of different members within the organisation. This knowledge can be shared with others to help develop the team or used to ensure that realistic decisions are made.

- **Explicit knowledge** is knowledge learned from books, teaching or research. There will be members within the team who have different qualifications or who have studied different things. Again, you will need to review this for yourself and the rest of the team.

Availability of IT systems to support the process

In every organisation, there are IT systems in place to allow staff members to store and share information. For example, each organisation has intranets and databases to help you store and share information across the organisation. Each method will have different levels of security and access to ensure that only the staff members who need the information have it.

Organisational culture

An **organisational culture** is a system of shared assumptions, values and beliefs, which govern how people behave in organisations. You should identify the organisational culture where you work and consider its level of trust and willingness to share knowledge.

Suitability of engagement approaches

Consider how engaged people are in the task, process, project or organisation. If there is a lack of engagement, you may need to consider other ways to engage and motivate your team and others.

Behaviours B

Takes responsibility
– Drive to achieve in all aspect of work.

Link to the standard 🔗

Knowledge Area 1: Outcome Topic 3.2

Skills area S

Knowledge Area 1: Outcome Topic 3.1

Key term 🔑

Organisational culture
– System of shared assumptions, values and beliefs, which govern how people behave in organisations.

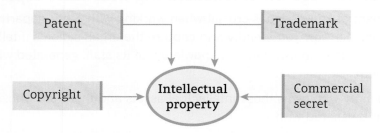

Identify intellectual property within your organisation.

Intellectual property

Intellectual property involves the creation of inventions, ideas, names and images used in business. It also involves any patents, copyrights or trademarks. Think about how you use these assets to ensure that you are not infringing any claims to intellectual property.

Collaborative technologies to manage knowledge

As well as IT systems to store and share information, you will also need to include collaborative technologies. These are forms of technology allowing different members of the team to contribute wherever they are based, for example Dropbox or Google Drive.

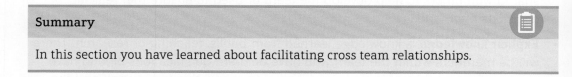

Summary

In this section you have learned about facilitating cross team relationships.

Activities

▶ **Activity 1**

Consider your personal and social skills. Make a list of those you have and those you need to develop. How will you develop these skills?

▶ **Activity 2**

Find out about the different laws and legislation protecting against discriminatory behaviour in the workplace.

How do they affect you in your role?

What do they require you to do?

Find out about your organisation's policy regarding discriminatory behaviour.

What procedures do you need to follow?

Who do you need to report it to?

Think of ways you can promote behaviour amongst your team that protects against discrimination and promotes equality and diversity.

▶ **Activity 3**

Think of a situation of conflict that has occurred in the workplace. This could be a situation you have been involved in or one that has occurred within your team. Reflect on the conflict and consider:

What caused the conflict? You may want to refer Bell and Hart's eight causes of conflict.

Could it have been avoided?

What did you do to try and resolve it?

What went well? What didn't?

What techniques could you use next time?

▶ **Activity 4**

Research the General Data Protection Regulations (GDPR). Consider how this will impact on how you collaborate with others in the workplace and how you share information.

▶ **Activity 5**

Consider the knowledge you have about your role, the organisation, its products or services or the industry you work in.

Divide it into two lists: tacit and explicit knowledge .

Where are the gaps in your knowledge?

Who else in the organisation has this knowledge?

How can you fill in the gaps in your knowledge?

Topic consolidation

▶ Test yourself

Use these questions to help you reflect on your understanding and experience and identify areas you need to develop.

1. How often are you upset and frustrated at work:

    ☐ never
    ☐ rarely
    ☐ sometimes
    ☐ often

2. In times of conflict, are you:

    ☐ calm and in control
    ☐ stressed and anxious
    ☐ out of your comfort zone
    ☐ relaxed and detached?

3. When considering your own emotional intelligence, do you:

    ☐ consider others' opinions of you
    ☐ control your own emotions
    ☐ reflect on your own performance
    ☐ slow down and make reasoned decisions?

4. Substantive conflict is:

    ☐ conflict around performance or the completion of tasks.
    ☐ conflict due to organisational regulations.
    ☐ conflict over how to achieve a goal or resolve a problem.
    ☐ conflict over how to achieve a goal or resolve a problem.

5. Think of a time where you had to deal with a situation of trivial conflict. Did you:

    ☐ not intervene
    ☐ negotiate to achieve a resolution
    ☐ intervene, reporting it to your manager
    ☐ hold a meeting to facilitate a resolution?

6. When working with other teams or departments, should you:

    ☐ agree and share common goals
    ☐ prioritise the interests of your team
    ☐ assume that everyone can work together
    ☐ ensure that you build trust between the teams?

4

Communication

What is communication?

Good communication is vital to working effectively as a team leader or supervisor. Communicating well can be difficult but will help you manage your team.

In this section you will find out about the methods of communication and how to overcome barriers to communication. You will learn about:

- different forms of communication
- organising meetings
- handling difficult conversations.

Methods of communication

Key terms

Verbal communication – The sharing of information between individuals by speech.

Body language – The use of movement or posture to communicate attitudes and feelings.

Communication involves sending and receiving information. This can be done by using either **verbal communication** or **body language**. You need to think carefully about how you use verbal communication and body language to ensure that you are communicating information effectively to your team. You also need to think about the format you will use and the communication channel the message will pass through to reach the person it is meant for. The way you communicate in a work environment is different to the way you communicate with your friends and family. It might feel strange communicating in a more formal way at first, so it is important to practise the skills involved to help you communicate in a professional manner.

Verbal communication

When working in teams we mostly communicate verbally. How we communicate verbally with others affects how the message is received and it is important that we do this effectively when leading a team. When communicating verbally consider the factors show in figure 1.

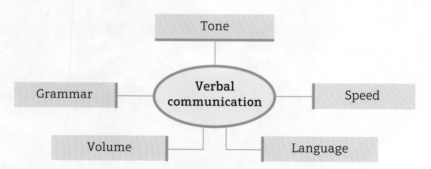

Figure 1: What types of verbal communication do you use at work?

Tone The tone of our voice is crucial when we communicate. If we sound aggressive or bad-tempered, this can stop people listening to and understanding the message.

Speed If we speak too quickly, this may cause parts of the message to be missed or misunderstood. However, talking too slowly can be frustrating for the listener and can make the communication ineffective.

Language When communicating verbally at work, it is important to use formal and professional language so your team understand that you are in a position of authority. Try and avoid slang terms and jargon or technical language that others might not understand.

Volume It is also key to consider the volume at which you speak, especially when the messages you are giving include sensitive information. Talking too quietly can mean that messages are not fully received but equally, talking too loudly can be disruptive in the work environment.

Grammar When communicating in the work environment use correct grammar. This helps ensure the message you are communicating is professional and creates a positive image of you and your company.

Body language

Body language is significant when communicating with others. This involves using your posture and movement to convey a message. You need to consider how to use body language effectively to help you communicate with your team.

What body language are you conscious of using?

Facial expressions Frowning or smiling when talking to people makes a difference to how they interpret what you are telling them. If want to give a serious message or instruction it helps to have a serious facial expression at that time; if you want to appear open and approachable, smiling encourages people to want to talk to you.

Eye contact Making eye contact with colleagues when you talk to them is important in gaining their trust and getting them to listen to what you have to say.

Gestures Using hand gestures can help to explain what you mean and engage others in your conversation. It is also a good way of providing information quickly, for example, pointing at something to draw someone's attention to it.

Posture The way you stand or sit can help people take you seriously. If you slouch in your seat or at your desk, people may not listen to you when you offer them instructions or ask them to do something.

Touch You must be careful in using touch to convey a message within the workplace. Innocent or well-meant forms of encouragement, such as a pat on the back, could be misconstrued as unwanted attention.

Summary

This is all about communication so now you know how to do it.
- Use verbal communication effectively to help you communicate with your team.
- Use body language to help communicate messages to your team.
- Understand how communicating effectively will help you lead your team.

Communication process

Any communication you undertake involves the same process, shown in figure 2 and table 1. The message is sent from the source to the recipient using an appropriate communication channel. However, some barriers to communication (noise) can get in the way, making the communication less effective. You need to understand how the communication process works and how to avoid the noise to help you communicate in the best way possible.

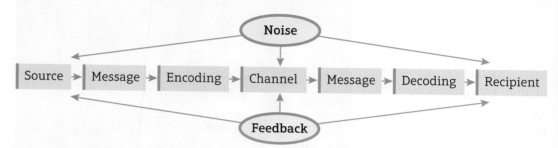

Figure 2: Think about how you communicate in the workplace. How does it follow this process?

Source	The source initiates the conversation.
Message	The source decides upon the message and the channel to be used.
Encoding	The source uses verbal communication and body language to send the information as a message.
Channel	The source chooses the communication – they can use verbal, written or online formats.
Decoding	The receiver interprets the message and tries to understand it.
Receiver	The receiver is the person who the message is intended for.
Feedback	Feedback is the final step, when the receiver sends information back to the source and vice versa.
Noise	The noise is the barrier to communication that may get in the way of the messages being received and understood.

Table 1: The stages of communication

Communication needs and requirements

Before you communicate with others in the workplace consider the purpose of the communication. Is it to pass instructions quickly onto a team member or to gather their ideas for a new project? The purpose of the communication will help you consider the appropriate communication method to use. In some organisations you may find that there are protocols in place, requiring you to communicate in a certain way. For example, if you need to communicate with other members of your team to organise a meeting, your employer may require you to do this in a written format, such as an email outlining the items for the agenda.

You will also need to consider the language you use. Your employer will expect you to be professional at all times and use language that is appropriate for the workplace. You need to remember that at all times at work you are representing your employer and you must consider the language you use. Sometimes, not thinking about the way we phrase instructions, ideas or feedback can upset other people and this could mean that you harm the working relationship you have with your team.

Customers have expectations of the company you work for and you will need to make sure you meet these expectations at all times. Customers will expect you to be polite and welcoming when you communicate with them, so you need to practise to ensure that you communicate appropriately with customers.

Communication channels

Communication is passed through a number of different channels in any organisation and you will need to be able to identify the different communication channels in your organisation and learn to communicate appropriately in each channel.

What is the communication chain of command in your workplace?

Direct communication This occurs when a message is transmitted from its source (the organisation) directly through a distribution channel to the receiver without anyone else involved or a noise. Examples include emails, letters or in person within face-to-face meetings.

Indirect communication This occurs when a message is transmitted from the source through another person to the receiver. There is a risk here that the intermediary person could misinterpret or misrepresent the information and therefore the message will not be clear or accurate when it is received.

Chain of command Communication is passed through the chain of command up and down the hierarchy. This is where information is cascaded down from senior management into teams and vice versa.

Summary

This is all about communication so now you know how to:

- understand how communication works
- consider how the needs and requirements of communication affect the choice of method used
- identify the communication channel being used to send the message.

Communication formats

Communicating effectively is dependent on selecting the correct format. You will use three main formats of communication.

1. Verbal formats – e.g. face-to-face, telephone, conference call, recorded

2. Written formats – e.g. letter, report, bulletin, poster, agenda, minutes, spreadsheets, tables, receipts, invoices, flyers, emails

3. Online format – social media, internet, intranet

There are advantages and disadvantages of using each of these formats that you need to consider before choosing to use them in the workplace; see table 2.

Format	Advantages	Disadvantages
Verbal	Saves time Flexible Creates a rapport	Emotions can distort the message No record Easy to forget the message
Written	Provides a record Easy to present complex information Formal image created	Expensive Time consuming Delay in response
Online	Cost effective Widespread audience Convenient	Can be outdated Text-based so can exclude some people Information overload

Table 2: Advantages and disadvantages of communication formats

Factors that affect the choice of communication media

When deciding on what form of communication media to use, there are a number of factors and questions that you will need to consider.

Audience How large, small, near, far, dispersed, etc. are the intended recipients?

Purpose Is the purpose, nature and tone of the communication **formal**, **informal**, critical or routine, etc?

Cost What is the most cost efficient way of transmitting the information to the intended recipients?

Speed How urgently should the information be transmitted and received?

Subject matter How complex, commercially valuable or sensitive is the communication?

Volume How much information is there to be transmitted?

Feedback Does the sender require a direct response from the recipient?

Record Does the sender need a record of the communication to provide evidence of it taking place?

Intrusion How intrusive or disruptive is the communication method?

Accuracy Does the communication contain precise and detailed information?

Key terms

Formal – Communication via the official channels in the organisation.

Informal – Communication through unofficial channels such as rumours, gossip and chats at the coffee machine.

Barriers to communication

In the communication process, you will encounter noise or barriers to communication. To ensure that you communicate well with your team and create good relationships, you will need to identify potential barriers to communication and find ways to overcome them; see figure 3.

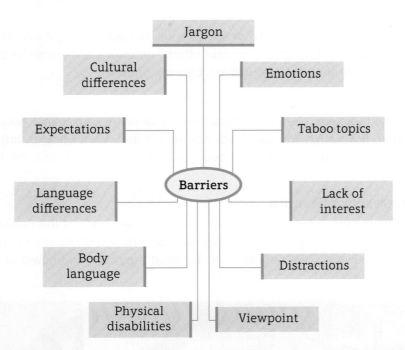

Figure 3: What barriers to communication might you face in your role as a team leader or supervisor?

Use of jargon

Using technical language or terms when communicating to others in the workplace could be confusing. Remember to think before you communicate about what words the recipient will understand and explain any technical terms to ensure that they understand you.

Emotions

If you or others are feeling stressed or upset, your message may get distorted or misunderstood. Be aware of your own and others' emotions and consider the best way to communicate the message without causing offence.

Taboo topics

Sometimes the topic you need to discuss may be sensitive or one that people are uncomfortable discussing. You will need to think carefully about how to introduce the topic and consider finding somewhere quiet, away from others to help the recipient feel comfortable.

Lack of interest or relevance

Even though you may understand the importance or relevance of the message, others may not be as interested. They may consider the information you are sharing to be irrelevant. Take time to consider what they need to know and remove anything unnecessary.

How do you communicate information to your team?

Distraction In the workplace there are distractions that impede communicating effectively with your team. Move the conversation to a quieter area to minimise distractions. Before you start a conversation, make sure that you and the recipient are able to give it your full attention.

Perception and viewpoint Others will not always share your viewpoint and may perceive something in a different way. You need to consider differing viewpoints and either change their point of view or explain that while they may disagree, you are still taking the action that you feel is right.

Physical disabilities Some of the people you work with or customers may have hearing or speech impairments. In this instance, you must think about how best to communicate. Checking that they have understood the message may help ensure effective communication.

Body language Inappropriate body language prevents effective communication. Consider what your body language says to the person you are talking to. Does it say that you are interested or bored? Do you seem aggressive or too laid back?

Language differences People in your team may have English as a second language. You will need to plan for this and consider how you will overcome the language barrier.

Expectations and prejudices We can have preconceived ideas about colleagues and customers and have expectations and prejudices that get in the way of communicating effectively. Treat everyone with the same respect and consideration. Do not assume something about someone or confine them to a stereotype.

Cultural differences If you work internationally or with people from different cultures, some differences may encumber effective communication. Develop your cultural awareness of different values and behaviours and act accordingly.

Methods to overcome barriers to communication

Once you have identified potential or actual barriers to communication, you will need to find ways to avoid them. Here are some tips to consider.

- Focus on the receiver and avoid distractions.

- Take the receiver and their needs more seriously.

- Give a crystal-clear message – practise it in advance if that helps.

- Consider the technique used to deliver the message to ensure that it is skillfully delivered.

- Use multiple channels to deliver the message so you know it is received and understood.

- Be aware of and control your own emotions and attitudes.

- Understand and prepare for the needs and background of the audience.

- Use the seven Cs of communication as shown in figure 4.

Behaviours B

Professionalism –
Open and honest.

Link to the standard

Knowledge Area 1:
Outcome Topic 4.1

Knowledge Area 1:
Outcome Topic 4.2

Seven Cs of communication

Figure 4: How can you use the seven Cs of communication to help you communicate more effectively with your team?

Clarity – Be clear about the goal or purpose of your communication.

Credibility – Ensure information that you communicate is reliable, trustworthy and dependable.

Content – Only include content that is relevant and meaningful to what is being said.

Context – Consider the background and wider meanings of what is being said.

Continuity – Connect information in a logical, consistent and continuous manner.

Capability – Ensure that the recipients have the power or ability to do what is being asked.

Channels – Communicate using appropriate channels, relative to the significance of the message.

Impacts of ineffective communication

Ineffective or poor communication can have a serious impact on a business or organisation and make it more difficult for you to fulfil your role.

Increased errors and mistakes If your team do not understand what to do and how to do it, they will make errors. This can waste time and money, as well as having a negative effect on customers.

Poor decision-making If people misunderstand messages or lack important pieces of information, they can make decisions that may not be the best for the organisation.

Conflict and disagreement Poor communication can lead to conflicts and disagreement within a team which prevents the job being done effectively. As a team leader it will be your responsibility to resolve these issues, so try and avoid them in the first place.

Misunderstanding and confusion When communication is not clear, it leads to misunderstanding and confusion, which slows down tasks.

Lower efficiency If people constantly check messages and ask for clarification, this can lead to inefficiency and error.

Decreased employee morale Poor communication can be demotivating for employees, which may mean that they are less willing to work well for you as their team leader.

Describe the levels of morale in your organisation

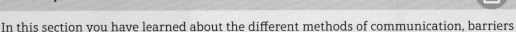

Summary

In this section you have learned about the different methods of communication, barriers to communication and how to overcome them. This section has covered:

- verbal communication and body language
- communication process
- communication needs and requirements
- communication channels
- verbal, written and online formats of communication
- factors affecting communication media choice
- impact of ineffective communication.

Organising and chairing meetings

As a team leader, you will have to organise and **chair** meetings with your team. This is an important aspect of your role and it is vital that you do this effectively. As the chair of the meeting you are responsible for leading and controlling the meeting, ensuring that everyone sticks to the **agenda** and all the items to be discussed are covered.

Preparation

In advance of the meeting, you will need to use a range of techniques to ensure that it is organised effectively. Remember that the more you can do in advance, the easier it will be to chair and control the meeting when it happens.

Preparation is the key to helping you be an effective meeting chair.

1. **Plan the agenda** You will find information on how to organise and plan the agenda later in this section.

2. **Discuss contributions to meeting** Discuss the requirements of any contribution to the meeting with other members of staff and agree what their contribution will involve. It is a good idea to provide times for their contribution to ensure that the pace of the meeting is maintained.

3. **Organise the date, time and venue** Agree a date and time, checking that all the staff contributing to the meeting can attend and then set up an appropriate venue for the meeting.

How can you improve the preparation for your meetings?

Improving preparations

1. List the staff to invite and check their availability before you send out invitations to the meeting. You will need to confirm who to invite.

2. Send out invitations to the meeting including the agenda and any additional information that needs to be read before the meeting. Collate this in advance from everyone who is contributing to the meeting.

3. Once you start to receive responses, you will need to collate them. Keep an ongoing list so you can check who has responded and who will attend the meeting. Chase up anyone who has not responded before the meeting date.

4. Make a final list of attendees so you know who to expect.

5. Make a record of staff not able to attend, so you are not waiting for them to start the meeting.

6. Once you have received any documents that have been prepared for the meeting, copy and distribute to all attending the meeting.

As chair of the meeting you have a number of responsibilities.

- Check everyone invited has arrived and signed in.
- Review the agenda.
- Outline the purpose of the meeting.
- Manage the order of the agenda.
- Control anyone dominating discussions.
- Control interruptions.
- Refocus the discussions where required.
- Set the pace of the meeting.
- Ensure the meeting keeps to time.

- Ensure all comments are addressed through the chair.
- Indicate progress made.
- Conclude one point before the next.
- Emphasise main points.
- Support the note taker.
- Clarify any misunderstanding.
- Summarise achievements and actions agreed.
- Arrange time and date of the next meeting.
- Sign off **minutes** of the meeting.

Key term

Minutes – Detailed notes that are taken during formal meetings to provide a record of what was discussed.

Techniques to facilitate meetings

You will need to develop a number of techniques to effectively facilitate meetings. These may be before the meeting takes place or during the meeting itself. It is important to consider and practise these techniques to ensure that your meeting works effectively.

Request advice or feedback from others in your organisation as to how to do this, so you know that you are doing this correctly.

Organising the agenda

Make sure that you organise the agenda in advance, allowing time for others to review and add to it, to ensure that you have a clear agenda to follow in the meeting. This will keep the meeting flowing and avoid any distractions or irrelevant discussions. You will need to:

- include the items to be covered
- include next to each item, the name of the member/s of staff responsible for reporting on this item
- allocate sufficient time to discuss each item
- provide a logical order to the items.

During the meeting

It is your role to effectively manage and control the meeting. It is vital that the meeting runs to plan and achieves its objectives. To do this, you will need to do the following.

Set clear expectations At the start of the meeting outline what the meeting is designed to achieve and also the behaviour of the staff attending. This ensures that everyone sticks to the focus of the meeting and behaves appropriately.

Manage time and relevance Check that the meeting runs to time. You might need to encourage the pace of those contributing and keep them informed of the time they have left. You also need to ensure that all the discussions are relevant to the agenda.

Intermittent summaries to keep on track At regular points during the meeting, review the discussion and suggest the next discussion point to keep the meeting on track.

Formalise agreements and actions During the meeting, certain actions will be agreed. Formalise these actions into the minutes of the meeting and highlight who is responsible for each action.

Manage disagreements In meetings, there are sometimes disagreements between staff. You need to manage these disagreements and ensure that they are resolved or left to one side to ensure that the meeting progresses.

Summarise agreed actions At the end of the meeting, summarise the agreed actions to ensure that they are recorded accurately, and all staff involved know what they are responsible for and by when.

Arrange next meeting Often another meeting will be required to review progress or discuss further items. You will need to agree the date, time and venue of the next meeting to ensure that all staff know when they are next expected to meet.

There will also be other of types of information, documentation and support required by the attendees of the meeting. You will need to consider these and ensure that you meet these requirements as chair of the meeting; see table 3.

Before a meeting:
publish the date, time and location of meeting
provide an agenda
offer any travel alternatives necessary
provide information about venue facilities.
During a meeting:
produce an attendance list for signing in
issue name badges for all attendees
distribute copies of the agenda
provide spare copies of documentation
ensure that contributor's presentation materials are available.
After a meeting:
share the minutes of the meeting
check on the results of actions given at the meeting
ask for progress reports on actions
request completion details of actions
request further consultations to develop targeted actions
identify any necessary amendments made to target action
make arrangements for next meeting.

Table 3: What does organising a meeting entail?

Behaviours

Inclusive – Seeks views of others. Open, approachable, authentic and able to build trust with others.

Link to the standard

Knowledge Area 1: Outcome Topic 4.2

Knowledge Area 1: Outcome Topic 4.1

Summary

In this section you have learned about how to organise and chair meetings. This section has covered:

- the role and responsibilities of the chair
- techniques to facilitate meetings
- information, documentation and support for meeting attendees.

Holding difficult conversations and knowing when to raise concerns

As a team leader you will sometimes have challenging conversations with members of your team. You may have to discuss under-performance or highlight issues with their behaviour and attitudes at work. Sometimes you will need to handle issues yourself, but you also need to be realistic and decide if and when to raise concerns about your team members to your manager or supervisor.

Key terms

Grievance – Complaint about unfair treatment in the workplace.

Discipline – The identification of unacceptable behaviour or conduct by a supervisor or manager, requiring improvements in behaviour.

Link to the standard

Knowledge Area 1: Outcome Topic 4.1

Knowledge Area 1: Outcome Topic 4.2

Holding challenging conversations

You may need to handle a challenging conversation for a number of reasons.

Addressing poor performance or conduct When identifying issues with poor behaviour or the conduct of members of your team, it is vital to address them as early as you can to ensure that behaviour or conduct is improved.

Dealing with personal problems Some of your team may be dealing with personal problems and you will need to discuss this with them to help support them. You may find the matters discussed make you feel uncomfortable and out of your comfort zone.

Investigating complaints You will need to investigate any complaints made about members of your team and help decide whether the complaints are upheld or unfounded.

Dealing with grievances and discipline Occasionally, employees may report **grievances** of unfair behaviour about colleagues. You will have to discuss this with different members of staff and you may have to **discipline** those who demonstrate poor behaviour or conduct.

Comfort or reassure someone A member of your team may be upset or need some reassurance. You may find this difficult, but being empathetic demonstrates that you understand how they feel.

Tackle personality clashes Whenever we work in teams, there are times when people don't get along and their personalities clash. As the team leader or supervisor, you will need to ensure that the team can work together.

Manage change Organisations can undergo many changes and you will be responsible for managing these within your team. This may mean that you have challenging conversations with your team, and implement the changes, regardless of how they feel about them.

To help you handle challenging conversations, you should prepare for the discussion in advance.

You will need to follow the process in figure 5.

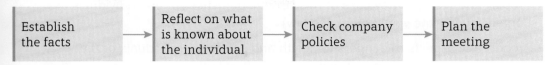

Figure 5: How could you use this process in preparing for difficult meetings?

Follow the framework for managing difficult meetings during your conversation. You may need to practise this. Include in your portfolio evidence of any meetings you have had like this to help you prepare for your professional discussion and competency-based interview.

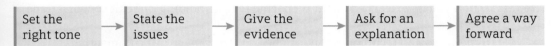

Figure 6: What can you do to set the right tone for this type of meeting?

Raising concerns and whistleblowing

Raising concerns to others within the organisation when you or one of your team members has identified an issue or a concern is your responsibility. Sometimes you will have to report these concerns even if you feel it is beyond your authority. Everyone has the responsibility to report anything that is unethical, illegal or deemed discriminatory. Failing to do so could damage an organisation's reputation and put your own or others' jobs at risk.

Every organisation will have its own reporting structure to report concerns to someone who will investigate and act if required; they will also have a **whistleblowing** policy. Though you may never need to use the policy it is important for you and your team to be aware of it and understand it. Employees need to be reassured that whistleblowing is without any implications for them in their role. Knowing the correct procedure ensures that you do not break company policy.

Any employee has the responsibility by law to disclose certain pieces of information.

Key term

Whistleblowing – Reporting the behaviour or actions of wrongdoing to the employer or relevant organisation.

Employees are expected to:

- disclose at the point of accepting a contract of employment any criminal offences on their record or any that are pending or being investigated

- report and testify in any case of miscarriage of justice (where individuals or organisations knowingly break the law)

- report any aspects of dangers to health and safety by individuals or the organisations to the relevant member of staff or authority

- report any damage to the environment to the relevant member of staff or authority

- report any deliberate attempt to conceal any of the aspects mentioned above.

Summary

In this section you have learned about preparing for and holding difficult conversations. In particular:

- the frameworks and techniques that can be used to manage difficult meetings
- knowing when and how to raise concerns and whistleblowing.

Activities

▶ **Activity 1**

Communication means taking in your environment and making sense of it. Create a table to outline the people you have spoken to recently. Were they good or bad experiences? If you are using an online portfolio you could also, with permission, create an image of your working environment and the policies and procedures you work around.

▶ **Activity 2**

Think about a message you have had to share with your team recently or one which you need to share in the near future.

- What barriers of communication could prevent the communication being effective?
- How could you plan to avoid them?
- Use the seven Cs of communication to help you in your plan.

▶ **Activity 3**

Think back to a difficult meeting you have had recently.

Make notes to explain how the approaches covered in this section could have helped you handle the meeting.

▶ **Activity 4**

Research the General Data Protection Regulations (GDPR). Consider how this will impact on how you collaborate with others in the workplace and how you share information.

▶ **Activity 5**

Find out what the reporting structure is in your own organisation and identify where you can go to raise any concerns you or your team have.

Topic consolidation

▶ Test yourself

1. Today were you:

    ☐ happy
    ☐ sad
    ☐ indifferent
    ☐ grumpy?

2. When communicating with a customer, were you:

    ☐ positive
    ☐ negative
    ☐ assertive
    ☐ passive?

3. When handling a challenging conversation, did you:

    ☐ listen to others' points of view
    ☐ assume the issues involved
    ☐ dominate the conversation
    ☐ respond immediately to the issues?

4. When having a meeting with your team, were you:

    ☐ under pressure because of time constraints
    ☐ unsure of your role
    ☐ clear in the setting expectations
    ☐ distracted by other aspects of your role?

5. Before a meeting do you need to:

    ☐ share an agenda
    ☐ produce an attendance list for signing in
    ☐ share the minutes of the meeting
    ☐ ask for progress reports on actions?

6. How happy would you be chairing a meeting tomorrow?

    ☐ very happy and confident
    ☐ somewhat happy and confident
    ☐ unhappy and not at all confident
    ☐ extremely unhappy and wouldn't feel confident

5

Operational management

What is organisational strategy?

An organisational strategy is the long-term vision and goals of what a company wants to achieve over a specific period and how they will plan and ensure it happens. This strategy is likely to be created by senior management. The vision, goals and plans are then cascaded through the management channels to operational staff. The whole of the company needs to be involved to ensure that strategic plans are fulfilled successfully.

Development of organisational strategy

Link to the standard

Knowledge Area 2:
Outcome Topic 1.1

Skills Area 2:
Outcome Topic 1.1

Knowledge Area 5.1:

Skills Area 5

Strategic plans

Long-term planning will focus on set periods of time over months and years, when an organisation will focus on its vision and priorities. A company will have a mission statement, explaining the purpose of the business, or why it exists. From the mission comes the company's vision, which describes what it wants to achieve to fulfil its mission. From the vision will come the long-term goals for organisational strategy.

Strategic management responsibility

Overall responsibility for strategic management will sit with the most senior managers of the organisation. This strategy will set a path for the business, guiding the company as it starts to implement its plans, evaluating and adjusting where necessary to ensure that the company stays focused and moving in the right direction. As a team leader or supervisor, you are likely to have been set goals by your manager. These will be part of the wider organisational strategic plan, and you have responsibility for managing your team to deliver these goals through a series of measurable actions.

The team leader's responsibility is likely to focus on one or more areas of the company strategic plan, depending on the structure of the organisation and the nature of the vision. However, all levels of management, including the team leader, should refer to the company strategic plan to guide them in their decision-making.

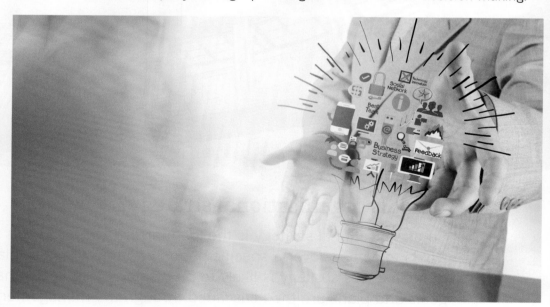

How does your organisational strategy fit with your own goals and objectives?

Behaviours **B**

Takes responsibility – Drive to achieve in all aspects of work.

Agile – Flexible to the needs of the organisation. Is creative, innovative and enterprising when seeking solutions to business needs. Positive and adaptable, responds well to feedback and need for change.

Professionalism – Open and honest. Operates within organisational values.

Developing an organisational strategy

There are several factors to consider when developing an organisational strategy, all of which are likely to be undertaken by senior management. Table 1 outlines how an organisational strategy might be developed.

Mission statement	Senior managers will create an official statement of the aims and objectives of the business. This will outline the purpose and definition of the business. The mission statement sets out the long-term aspirations of the organisation over at least the following year.
Objectives	Objectives must be SMART (Specific, Measurable, Achievable, Realistic and Time-bound). These will provide a focus and give a foundation for rational decision-making ensuring the process is achievable and effective. A reference point for final decisions and success criteria can then be easily identified.
Scope	Scope includes deciding on the level of decision-making: strategic, tactical or operational. Part of scoping out the organisational strategy is to decide who will make the decisions and whether they will be individual, group or organisational decisions. It is important that the scope is accurate to ensure that decisions are taken by the right people and that appropriate objectives and success criteria are identified.
Success criteria	Success criteria are the measures that determine the best possible outcomes of the organisational strategy. Where there are several options within the objectives, the most relevant and important factors should be used in determining their success. It is important to understand and know what the success criteria are as this will allow you to identify how each option has performed against each of the objectives. It will also help to ensure that decisions made meet the identified objectives.

Table 1: How would you develop an organisational strategy?

Framework and basis for lower-level planning

The organisational strategic plans need to be broken down into manageable and achievable lower-level plans often referred to as tactical or operational plans. These plans will have shorter timescales with 'milestone' achievement tasks and dates that will support the overall organisational strategy.

Depending on the size and structure of your organisation, as a team leader you may be involved in creating a lower-level plan, or you may be given the plan by your manager. In either case, you need to ensure that you fully understand the content of the plan and are confident that you and your team can deliver it successfully. Table 2 is an example framework for lower-level planning.

Specific goals with fixed deadlines	These specific goals must be SMART for them to be achieved. For example, if a retailing company wishes to expand, it should state how many stores per month it will open, or what the percentage growth of business will be per month, etc.
Budgets	The plan should list what needs to be spent to achieve the goals. These costs should include all expenditure such as wages, marketing, purchasing and costs of running the day to day operations of the business.
Resources	The plan should list all the resources needed to fulfil the plan, which should feed into the budgets if there is a cost attached. These resources should include human resources as well as physical resources.
Marketing	Any marketing that may be required to achieve the goals must be listed and the costs estimated and added to the budgets.
Funding	The source of funding should be included on the plan to ensure that costs can be met, and the achievement of the lower-level plan can stay within budget.

Table 2: Lower-level planning

Link to the standard

Knowledge Area 2: Outcome Topic 1.1

Behaviours

Takes responsibility – Drive to achieve in all aspects of work.

Agile – Flexible to the needs of the organisation. Is creative, innovative and enterprising when seeking solutions to business needs. Positive and adaptable, responds well to feedback and need for change.

Professionalism – Open and honest. Operates within organisational values.

Summary

In this section you have learnt about how organisational strategy is developed and the internal/external influences on its development. This section has covered:

- strategic plans and management responsibility
- frameworks and basis for lower-level planning
- using models such as PESTLE and SWOT analysis.

External influences

There are several external and internal factors that can impact the development of an organisational strategy. External influences can be determined through the completion of a PESTLE analysis; this covers political, economic, socio-cultural, technological, legal and environmental issues. Table 3 gives some examples of each sector.

Political	Taxes, regulations, services
Economic	Inflation, stock market trends, unemployment
Socio-cultural	Population demographics, education, distribution of wealth
Technological	Innovation, infrastructure levels, communication
Legal	Data protection, health and safety laws, e-commerce
Environmental	Weather, climate change, energy

Table 3: Determine external factors using a PESTLE analysis

Benchmarking

Benchmarking is how an organisation compares its own products, services and ways of working with other businesses in their sector. It allows the organisation to determine if they are operating and performing effectively and efficiently and to the same standard, or better, than their competitors.

An organisation can measure their internal performance against an external standard to identify any improvements needed to remain competitive. Managers can also use benchmarking to establish best practice within their industry and ensure that organisational strategy meets or exceeds this measure.

SWOT analysis

SWOT analysis is an effective way for an organisation to understand its strengths and weaknesses and to identify the opportunities and threats it faces. Opportunities should be identified to build on the strengths and eliminate or reduce weakness. The questions an organisation asks within a SWOT analysis will vary according to the nature, values, culture and structure of the business.

Demographic influences

Demographics catagorise the social statistics of the human population. The composition of most populations is constantly changing and the speed at which these changes occur will vary from area to area and country to country. Organisations need to be aware of the demographic factors that make up their customer base and that can positively and negatively influence their business.

Organisational culture and values

An organisational strategy should align with the organisation's culture for it to be developed and implemented successfully. The vision and goals can only be effective when management and operational staff believe and demonstrate the same culture and values.

Implementing an operational or team plan

There are several components within an operational or team plan that need to be implemented to ensure that operations within the business are successful. These will help ensure the strategic goals are effectively met. These are shown in table 4.

Individual and team goals that include SMART objectives	Each team member has specific responsibilities and accountability in delivering their part of the team goal.
A list of activities and tasks to be completed	These keep the team focused and within their timescales. These should include team and individual tasks written into action or development plans. They should be constantly visible to the whole of the team and discussed regularly at team meetings.
The roles and responsibilities of team leader or supervisor and that of the team members	Each team member should clearly understand their role and responsibilities within the organisation. This can be communicated in a job description or terms of reference and should align with their day to day role. Performance measures and/or discrepancies can then be discussed at one-to-one meetings.
Performance measures or key performance indicators (KPI)	Performance measures should be in place for the team leader or supervisor and the team members. These should relate to goals and SMART objectives and linked to roles and responsibilities. By measuring an individual against KPIs, performance issues and development plans can be established, and good performance recognised and rewarded.
Resource requirements	The resources required to implement the operational or team plan must be identified and accounted for to ensure success. The team need to be equipped with the appropriate materials and costs identified to ensure they can be included in the budget.
Financial requirements	Sufficient finance must be available to implement an operational or team plan. All costs and possible expenditure must be identified and written into a budget. The organisation must have the funds available to meet the budget, through cash in the bank or through other means such as a loan.
A risk assessment and mitigation strategy	All projects have risks that need to be identified and managed. It is good practice to have a backup of alternative plans and solutions to keep plans on track.

Table 4: Have you implemented these components in your team plan?

Link to the standard

Knowledge Area 2:
Outcome Topic 1.2

Skills Area 2:
Outcome Topic 1.2

Key term

Mitigation – An action to reduce the severity or seriousness of something.

Performance objectives

The operational or team plan can be short to medium term and is made up of five performance objectives.

Cost

Here, the objective is looking at how the costs might change over time. This is dependent on supply and demand and the impact of increased production costs or lower selling price, both of which would affect profit.

Dependability

Can the organisation deliver products on time, meeting the planned prices and costs? The objective here is to determine how dependable the product or service is and if it can function consistently and as intended over time. If a product or service cannot meet the customer expectations or match the quality and reliability of competitors within budget, then it is not going to be dependable. This can lead to customer complaints and poor sales, weakening any plan.

Flexibility

How much flexibility has been built into the operational plan? In this objective, the organisation must cope with changes, such as new legal requirements to product lines or services to reflect changes in legislation, or health and safety.

Quality

How well do the organisation's products and/or services conform to the specifications? The organisation has to ensure its products and/or services are meeting the expected specification. The objective should also consider how desirable the features of the product and/or service are and its perceived value to potential customers. Reliability, durability and how well the product and/or service performs its function are also measures of quality that can be included in the objective.

Speed

How fast can the organisation deliver its products and generate sales? In this objective, the organisation is identifying the speed at which their products and/or services can be generated to ensure quality and meet demand. The identified time required is then factored into the operation or team plan.

Each performance objective should be assessed as shown in figure 1.

Figure 1: Review these performance objectives in your organisation

It can be difficult for the whole of an organisation to work in the same way. However, it is important to achieve this consistency to support the effective implementation of an operational or team plan. The larger the company, the more difficult this can be. It is therefore important that the company mission, vision and core values are communicated to everyone in the organisation. Everyone must understand how their project fits into the larger organisation framework and how their specific contribution impacts company strategy; see figure 2. There are several ways to ensure that there is alignment across the workforce of an organisation.

- Employees receive consistent and continuous feedback related to their objectives and the overall company strategy.

- Tasks are allocated appropriately to ensure that each team member is fully aware of their role and responsibility and has, or can develop, the necessary skills set.

- Team members are recognised for their contribution and achievements. Making an employee feel valued is essential to keep them engaged and focused. Simply thanking them for their contributions and recognising when they have done a good job can be huge motivating factors. By showing an employee how their contribution and performance is helping to meet the company's overall objectives is likely to encourage more hard work and dedication.

Figure 2: How do your team fit within the wider organisation framework?

Managing resources

The managing of resources starts with identifying what will be required for a team to deliver their operational plan; see table 5. Once this has been established, you must manage the resources to ensure they are used appropriately and there is little wastage. The amount of resources required may fluctuate, depending on the workload. For example, in busy periods when there is a greater demand there is likely to be a need for a greater number of resources and vice versa.

Assess what is needed	The team leader or supervisor should involve their team when deciding what resources will be required to deliver the operational plan. This will ensure engagement and give shared responsibility in the accuracy of identifying the resources.
Cost resources and put into budget	Any resource needs to be costed accurately and entered onto the budget of the operational plan. Accurate costing and budgeting are essential to ensure that sufficient funds are available and costs are monitored to ensure that the operational plan stays within the budget.
Research suppliers	Part of the operational plan will be to source the best suppliers. Factors contributing to this selection will include: cost of product and carriage, discounts for large orders or early payment, credit terms, quality of product, availability of product, delivery times, reputation of the supplier and any existing relationship between the organisation and the supplier, etc.
Order and/ or install the resources	Once the supplier has been chosen, items then need to be ordered and where appropriate installed. This will take coordination and planning to ensure the resources are ready to be used and fit within the operational plan's timescales.
Assess and cost in regular maintenance of electrical checks	Some of the resources required may need regular maintenance and/or electrical checks. These costs must be factored in and planned for, by including them in the budget of the operational plan.
Staff training	A training needs analysis should be completed to identify what training will be required for those working on the operational plan. There will be several areas to consider, such as training for specialist equipment or software applications.
Safety and security of equipment/ purchases	To ensure the safety and security of equipment, staff must be trained in how to use the equipment correctly. Equipment must be kept locked and secured where appropriate to avoid misuse and prevent it being stolen. The costs of security and safety of the equipment and purchases need to be managed to keep preventable losses to a minimum.
Assess IT support that may be required	Resources are likely to include an element of IT, whether directly implementing a new system or indirectly when used as a communication channel. Involving the team and IT experts to assess the amount of IT needed in the project and any relevant support, will help identify how this can be managed as part of the operational plan.

Table 5: Have you considered which physical resources your team will need to carry out your organisation's operational plan?

Managing staffing

You may need to increase the size of your original team to deliver the operational or team plan; see table 6. As the team leader or supervisor, you are likely to discuss this with your own manager to establish how many people you need and on what terms. You may also be involved in the recruitment of new team members.

Workload dependency	The number of staff required to deliver the operational plan can be determined through careful consideration of the tasks to be completed. This must include the skills needed and the level of the employees. You may only need specific skills for a short period, for example if installing an IT system.
Meeting deadlines	Staff must be managed to ensure that they meet their individual target, which will help to meet the overall deadlines. Team members must be aware of their deadlines and encouraged to discuss any issues with their team leader or supervisor. The team leader must create an environment of trust and cooperation and conduct regular one-to-ones with each team member.
Full or part-time, contracted staff	There may be a need for full- and part-time staff to align with the workload as it builds and declines. The organisation should also consider the needs of the workforce, who may request a part-time role, to ensure it is adhering to employment law. It may be appropriate for specific roles to be filled by contractors who work for the organisation for a specific amount of time.
Recruitment procedures **Job descriptions/ specifications** **Liaising with HR**	Recruitment procedures will depend on the size of the organisation. Larger organisations will have an HR department, whereas smaller companies may rely on managers to undertake recruitment. When managing staffing resources, it is important that the team communicate to the correct person or department to ensure that they have enough staff with the appropriate skills-set to be able to deliver the operational plan.
Induction training	When new team members are recruited, they will need to undertake a company induction. This will include training around the organisation's systems and procedures and possibly the skills required for their new role, depending on the competence of the individual and the nature of the role. As the team leader, you may be part of the induction training to ensure that your new team member completes their induction to become an effective member of the team.
Integration into the team	In some organisations a mentor is allocated to new members of staff to help them settle in. It will be your role as the team leader to ensure a smooth integration into the team. Regular communication with the new team member is essential.
Absence, illness, annual leave	Planned absence, such as holidays, can be managed in advance and organised into the operational plan to avoid disruption. However, unplanned absence, such as illness, is likely to require quick thinking and action as potential cover for an absence may be required. By having a contingency plan for such occasions, you can help to reduce the amount of disruption to the operational plan.

Table 6: Things to consider when determining how many people you will need

Monitoring resources

When implementing an operational or team plan it is important to monitor the different aspects of the resources.

Impact on the environment

Any negative impact on the environment needs to be monitored to reduce the effects. In some instances, there may be little to be done, whereas in other cases action can be taken that will either directly reduce any negative impact, or influence others to reduce any negative impact. For example, an organisation may choose to only work with partners who consider the impact on the environment or buy products that are less harmful to the environment.

Benefits and methods of waste reduction

Waste reduction is likely to result in a cost saving to the organisation, and so every effort should be made to reduce waste. Monitoring the amount of waste generated, making team members aware of areas of wastage and educating them on how it can be reduced will help in ensuring wastage is kept to a minimum. Opportunities for recycling and/or reusing products and materials should be discussed with the team to generate ideas and viable methods for reducing waste.

Remedial action

Key term

Remedial – To correct something that is wrong or improve a bad situation.

Things will not always go as originally planned and there may be times when **remedial** action is required to keep things on track. There may have been assumptions when planning, that were incorrect; in this situation the team leader should work with their manager and team to find effective solutions to these problems as quickly as possible. Continuous monitoring of the resources used during the implementation of a plan will allow the team leader to take remedial action to ensure the most appropriate and correct amount of resources are used in the most effective way.

Accurate records

it is essential that all records are accurate and are a true reflection of the exact stage an organisation is at within its operational plan. The team leader may have responsibility for monitoring some, or all, records such as accounts, budgets, payments, orders, staffing rotas, risk assessments, insurance documents, etc. Having accurate records means reports can be generated with precise information about the progress and success of organisational operations.

Service level agreements (SLA)

An SLA is a legally binding contract between the supplier (service provider) and the organisation (customer) receiving their services or goods. It sets out the agreed terms of business and services. There is usually a designated person managing the SLA for each of the parties who is the point of contact. The content of the SLA can include items such as scope and standard of goods or services supplied, supplier/customer responsibilities, penalties for breach of contract, etc. As team leader or supervisor, you may have responsibility in monitoring the SLA to ensure agreements are met.

Evaluating resources

Part of managing resources is evaluating their effectiveness both during and at the end of an operational plan. Figure 2 shows the factors you need to consider. This will help an organisation establish which the most useful resources were, which they could forget in similar projects or how the resources might be used more effectively.

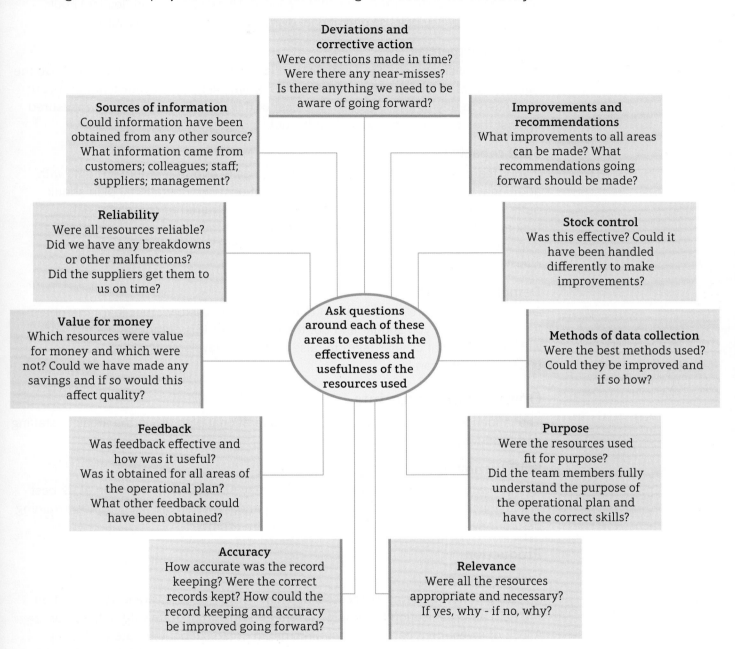

Figure 3: How effective and useful are your resources?

Staffing

Staffing levels

It may be difficult to recruit or retain staff. In both cases this will impact the operational plan. Talking to your team regularly and planning will help to mitigate some of the problems arising from issues with staffing levels. However, the team leader should have a contingency plan, so operational disruption is kept to a minimum.

Access to expertise

When specialist jobs need to completed, it is important that team members have the right skills set. There may be a shortage of certain skills within your team and you may need to buy in this expertise. The cost of this expertise needs to be measured against the speed and accuracy that it would bring to the project or task.

Staff capacity

If your team is already working at their full capacity and they would struggle with additional tasks then this will impact on operations. The operational plan should outline a calculated or estimated amount of time required to complete each task against the number of staff available and the time they have. There may be opportunities to offer overtime, or your organisation may have a restriction on overtime hours.

Demotivated staff

Demotivated staff are likely to affect operations and possibly other team members. As a team leader, you should find out the reasons for this demotivation and work with the individual or your team to raise motivation levels, so your team are as effective as they can be.

Operational constraints

The influences that put constraints on the operational plan are in the areas of staffing and production.

Staff turnover

By not having enough staff, an organisation may not be able to function at its best or at capacity. However, recruitment is costly and new staff are likely to need training before they become effective and valuable team members.

Production

Lack of investment

Investing in new systems, processes, machinery, staff or other areas of production will help an organisation to remain current and able to operate within its sector. A lack of investment can put constraints on an organisation, ultimately affecting operations and the success of the organisation as it becomes outdated and unable to sustain a competitive market position.

Inability to implement an effective quality assurance system

Quality assurance in production is an important part of operations that ensures products and/or services are safe, reliable and fit for purpose. Costs are attached to a quality assurance process. However, without one in place it can lead to customer complaints and possibly unsafe or illegal working practices.

Inadequate supply of parts and raw materials

A constant and sufficient supply of parts and raw materials is essential to ensure production operations are not interrupted. It can be expensive for production to be halted and restarted and it will have a negative impact on the availability of goods and services to customers. The efficient management of stocktaking and ordering processes will help maintain an adequate supply of parts and/or raw materials to avoid interruption to production.

Limited capacity

There needs to be a balance between the amount of work required and the possible output that machinery and production staff can supply. There will be a maximum amount that a production line can produce and staff will have set hours each day in which to work. If this is not adequate to meet demand, there will be a constraint on operations, which will need to be managed and communicated back to the organisation.

Under-utilisation of machinery and equipment

If machinery and/or equipment is not being used to its maximum capacity, it will have an impact on the operations and success of the organisation. Costs to the organisation of purchasing and maintaining machinery and/or equipment will be made even if it is not used to capacity. While machinery and equipment is being used, it is contributing to the success and profits of the business; when it is under-utilised, it can be a potential cost to the business.

Summary

In this section you have learnt about how to implement operational or team plans and how to effectively manage resources. This section has covered:
- the different components to consider, such as individual and team goals
- performance objectives
- managing physical and staffing resources
- monitoring physical and staffing resources.

Approaches to managing change within the team

Link to the standard

Knowledge Area 2:
Outcome Topic 1.3

Skills Area 2:
Outcome Topic 1.3

The way in which changes are approached is likely to impact on the success of that change. By providing a positive and professional environment, the team leader can be effective while implementing any change. It will ensure the team have direction and processes can be driven forward. Team members are likely to become engaged and empowered to be a positive part of the change. This, in turn, can result in increased motivation, encouraging team members to complete tasks on time and adhere to budgets, and general staff effectiveness.

Types of change

When used effectively, change models will support the management of change. You should also consider who the change will affect and the risks involved in implementing the change. Table 7 shows some different types of change.

Step change	This is a large and sudden change generally occurring in one stage that is likely to improve things once the change has been fully implemented.
Incremental change	This is when change is made over several smaller steps until the desired change is complete. It will have less immediate impact but will take longer to achieve.
Planned change	The organisation can announce the change that is happening and establish a plan, so that each stage of the change can be communicated to all of those who will be affected.
Unplanned change	This may be a result of unexpected circumstances that the organisation was not expecting but needs to react to.

Table 7: Types of change

Change management models

Lewin's 3-stage change model

This model looks at the human aspects and factors for and against change; see figure 4.

Figure 4: Lewin's 3-stage change model

Change is seen as a process rather than an event. Establishing stability can be difficult, if another change is imminent. The process goes through the following three stages.

1. **Unfreeze** The organisation prepares the workforce to accept that change is necessary. This part of the process can be challenging and the most stressful as the organisation seeks cooperation and buy-in from staff.

2. **Change** Following the uncertainty that the unfreeze stage brings, the workforce can begin to change their behaviour and accept the change. To do this, they will need to know how the change will benefit them and the organisation. Individuals will arrive at this stage of the change at different times, or not at all. The team leader must manage individuals and not assume that everyone in the team will embrace change in the same way or at the same time.

3. **Refreeze** Once the change has taken place, the organisation needs to 'refreeze' by ensuring policies and procedures are in place to reflect and reinforce the change.

Kotter's 8-step change model

This model takes a holistic approach to a planned change by initially creating an urgency to finally anchoring the changes in the corporate culture; see figure 5. This model focuses on staff buy-in as the **catalyst** for success. While it identifies clear steps, Kotter's model can lead to frustration if staff members' needs are not considered. It is a top-down model that fits in well with traditional organisational hierarchies.

Key term

Catalyst – A person or event that causes a change.

1	Create an urgency
2	Form a coalition
3	Create a vision for change
4	Communicate a vision
5	Remove any obstacles
6	Create short-term wins
7	Build on these wins
8	Anchor the change

Figure 5: Kotter's 8-step change model

1. **Create an urgency** Using open and honest conversations will help most, if not all, team members to understand the importance of acting and the need for change.

2. **Form a coalition** By creating a project team of individuals who have embraced the need for the change it will support the change by having a team with a cooperative and constructive approach.

3. **Create a vision for change** This will help everyone see what the organisation is trying to achieve by implementing the change.

4. **Communicate the vision** Everyone within the organisation needs to be aware of the vision for change and should be given the opportunity to voice their opinions, concerns and any anxieties.

5. **Remove any obstacles** By having an open dialogue with team members, it will help you to establish who might be resistant to the change. By listening to them, you can act to reduce or remove any obstacles.

6. **Create short-term wins** Success is a great motivator, and so any early successes are likely to be received positively by the team and motivate them to continue until the change is complete.

7. **Build on the short-term wins** Once the first short-term wins have been successful, you should increase the pace of the change to maintain and boost momentum.

8. **Anchor the changes** The change will only be successful once it becomes recognised as normal practice within the organisation. The organisation should align its values, standards and update processes to the changes and as team leader you should support and reinforce the change.

Kubler-Ross 5-stage model

This model captures the individual's reaction to change, which follows a 5-stage change path of emotions; see figure 6. This includes denial, where the individual does not want to believe that the change is happening, to anger where the individual is angry about the change, to bargaining where the individual offers alternatives and/or solutions so that the change does not need to happen, to depression where the individual feels 'down' about the idea of change to finally acceptance that the change is here to stay.

Figure 6: Kubler-Ross 5-stage model

This model assumes the worse reaction to change and it can be difficult to identify the transition between each phase of the change path. It can therefore be difficult to use this model with a group of people.

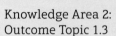

Link to the standard

Knowledge Area 2: Outcome Topic 1.3

Summary

In this section you have learnt about the approaches to managing change within a team. This section has covered:

- types of change, including step change, incremental change, planned and unplanned change
- change management models including Lewin's 3-stage change, Kotter's 8-step change and Kubler-Ross 5-stage change models
- the roles of stakeholders during the change period
- risks and how to manage risks associated with change.

The role of stakeholders during change

Different levels of commitment and support will be required by both internal and external stakeholders to ensure the success of any change within an organisation.

- **High level of commitment** This will be active and visible support that you identify as crucial to successful implementation of the change.

- **Medium level of commitment** This is where the stakeholders' support and commitment are important to the change, but not crucial.

- **Low level of commitment** At this level, implementation of the change is likely to be successful without the support of the stakeholder, although their involvement would be welcome.

Link to the standard

Knowledge Area 2: Outcome Topic 1.3

It is important that you identify your internal and external stakeholders and the level of commitment that you require from them, and that you communicate the role that you would like them to play.

The RACI model, see table 8, is a useful tool for identifying who will have responsibility and accountability for the tasks required during a change. This will also include who will need to be consulted and informed. Table 9 shows an example of the RACI model.

R	**Responsible** R is used to identify who is responsible for the implementation of a task and that it is delivered on time.
A	**Accountable** A is used to identify the person who is accountable for the accurate completion of each task. There should only be one person who is ultimately accountable and this should be the person who will sign off a task as complete.
C	**Consulted** C is used to identify the people whose opinion is required and therefore there will be a two-way conversation and ongoing communication.
I	**Informed** I is used to identify the people who you need to keep up to date on the progress and decisions made for each task. This is likely to be a one-way communication.

Table 8: Responsibility assignment matrix

Task	Stakeholder 1	Stakeholder 2	Stakeholder 3	Stakeholder 4
Task 1	R	I	C	I
Task 2	C	A	C	A
Task 3	I	A	R	I
Task 4	A	I	I	C

Table 9: Example of a RACI model to identify the stakeholders within your own organisation and establish their roles/responsibilities

Risks associated with change

Link to the standard

Knowledge Area 2:
Outcome Topic 1.3

When managing a change within the organisation, you should identify and assess any likely risks to the business so that you can put a plan in place to either remove or reduce the risk. Having a contingency option in place will help you and your team to be able to make quick decisions should the risk arise to keep the change on course and moving forward.

Types of risks that may threaten change within an organisation include are explored below.

Active and/or passive resistance to the change

Your team may be reluctant to accept new systems or procedures and have little faith in the process, especially if they feel they do not have enough knowledge to understand how the change will affect them. Their personal preferences may mean they do not like the changes being introduced or they may think the change presents a risk to their job. Team members' behaviours will all be different and either active or passive. In both cases, you should talk to your team to reassure them and involve them in the change, so that they take ownership, feel valued and can see the benefits of the change.

Ineffective leadership

Leadership can be ineffective because of a lack of experience in managing change or due to a lack of training. If you are managing change for the first time, ask for support and additional training so that you can be an effective leader. Keep focused on the change and make it your priority.

Disruption to the operation of the business

Any change can mean an amount of disruption to the business. When you are managing a change, identify the severity of the disruption the change is likely to cause, and the timescales involved, before the disruption is over. There may also be a financial impact, which may be a risk to the business due to additional costs resulting from implementing the change.

Key term

Inception – The starting point of a project or plan.

Enforcing the change

If change is forced through it may not be seen by the workforce as needed. There may be a lack of understanding as to why the change is happening, if your team have not been involved in the process from **inception**. It is important that they are engaged and feel empowered throughout any change.

Managing the risk associated with change

Asking appropriate questions is essential if you are to manage any risks effectively.

The types of questions you might ask include those shown in figure 7:

Link to the standard

Knowledge Area 2: Outcome Topic 1.3

Is the speed in which the change is being adopted appropriate?

Is the business meeting the change objectives?

Will completion of the change be timely?

Will the returns from the change be lower than anticipated?

Questions

Is the business being disrupted by the change and if so, what are these disruptions?

Will the change come in on budget?

Figure 7: What other questions might you ask to reduce the risks to the change you are managing?

Contingency planning

Asking the right questions will allow you to think about what you can put in place should something go wrong. This will enable you to be proactive in planning for both predictable events and events out of your control. This would include events outside the range of normal operations of your organisation that might **adversely** affect your organisation's ability to operate.

By having a contingency plan, any critical activities can be identified and any that are at risk can be highlighted; any need for change of direction can then be brought forward and quickly put into action. A contingency plan can also identify resources and procedures needed to carry out operations during any prolonged interruptions to normal operations.

Key term

Adversely – In a way that is harmful or prevents achievement.

Data management

Different types of data will be required, depending on the required outcome of the results. The three types of data, their usage and limitations are described in table 10 on the next page.

Business data

This is the data required by the organisation to support operations and inform on business decisions. It can be used to benchmark performance, promote efficiency and help support the development of a competitive advantage over other organisations in the same business sector. There are limitations that need to be considered when using business data, which should be tested and double-checked to ensure its accuracy and reliability. Data may be misinterpreted, or it may be interpreted in a way towards a specific bias in favour of the view of an individual or department.

Link to the standard

Knowledge Area 2: Outcome Topic 1.4

Key terms

Benchmark – A point of reference by which something may be compared.

Bias – Favouritism towards or against something.

	Usage	Limitations
Business data	Support operations Inform business decisions **Benchmark** performance Promote efficiency Develop a competitive advantage Increase market share	Accuracy and reliability of data Misinterpretation of data Access to data Confidentiality of data Legal and regulatory issues **Bias** towards aspects of the data
Qualitative data	Descriptive information Relate to the quality of a service or process Data is personal and open to interpretation	Knowledge produced may not be applicable to other settings Difficult to make quantitative predictions Difficult to test hypotheses and theories with last participant pools Timescales involved in collecting data Ethical issues Subjectivity and bias
Quantitative data	Information measured in numbers, sizes or percentages Amenable to statistical manipulation	Accuracy and reliability of data Misinterpretation of data Bias towards certain aspects of the data Access and confidentiality Legal and regulatory issues

Table 10: Types of data

Qualitative data

This is data based on descriptive information from several sources and usually relates to the quality of a service, product or process. This type of data gives detailed information that can be open to interpretation and can be used to inform specifics, such as people's opinions and actions to be taken. The limitation to this type of data is that it may only be specific to one setting and so cannot be used for any other purpose. It is also difficult to make predictions from qualitative data as each piece of data is likely to be unique and will not necessarily identify any trends.

Quantitative data

This data is based on figures as it totals the numbers given within the data. For example, the data results may show percentages, numbers or sizes. When working with quantitative data it is possible to interpret the data in different ways, which may be useful to an organisation when they want to find out several possibilities from one set of data. The limitations of quantitative data are that its accuracy and reliability may be incorrect if the figures have not been entered correctly at the point of original input; it is also open to misinterpretation.

For all types of data, it is important to respect the confidentiality and access to the data to ensure that you are operating within the law and meeting data protection requirements. You should be aware of the way in which data is interpreted to avoid bias.

Validity and reliability of data

It is important that the data you gather comes from trusted sources. You should determine in advance the level of detail that will be required for the data to be meaningful and to allow you to make informed decisions and/or recommendations.

You will need to consider ownership of the data and how current it is. There is likely to be a cost to collecting the data and this should be factored into your budgets.

To ensure the data you collect is valid and reliable, it needs to be unbiased and a true representation of what or who you are gathering information from. When checking for validity and reliability you should make the considerations outlined in table 11.

Validity and reliability of data	Considerations
Bias	Are your samples representative of the population you have collected data from? Are you using leading questions, which could make them biased? Are focus groups run to ensure inclusion and participation from everyone? Are your questions written and structured to avoid influencing respondents? It is difficult to eliminate bias totally, however, you should be aware that your own attitude, behaviour and beliefs will have an impact too. Keep an open mind while collecting data and be aware of any bias.
Representative	Is the data collected a true representation? If you gather data from a small sample you must check that your results reflect the larger entity when they are scaled up.
Verifiable	Can you check the data to ensure that it is genuine and accurate? Any translation of the data or migration from one system to another must be completed accurately to ensure that it remains true to the original outcomes.
Accuracy	Have you used the correct methodology for collecting the data? Has the data been entered on the database accurately? Have you captured the appropriate target audience for collecting the data? Can you be sure any respondents have answered questionnaires honestly? The planning process should eliminate some inaccuracies. However, you should also check for accuracy as you gather the data, and as part of the data analysis.
Reliable, consistent and dependable	Is your approach and the way you have collected the data consistent? Can you trust the data sets to be an accurate representation? For example, if you are using a staff questionnaire to gather information and make changes to some of the questions in the survey then you will get a slightly different response to those from the original version. This will then make your data of the sample unreliable.
Stable	Has the data been recorded exactly as you intended it to be? Is it accurate and consistent?
Plausible	When checking your data, are any numbers or comments substantially different from your expectations? If your answer is yes, then your data needs to be checked for accuracy and reliability. Look for any errors that may have occurred, such as incorrect data input or misinterpretation of comments. You may also look at how the data was collected and where the responses came from so that you can check that the data is plausible.

Table 11: Considerations for checking validity and reliability of data

Issues relating to the analysis of data

There are several issues relating to the analysis of data that you must be aware of when following your organisation's procedures for collecting, analysing, presenting and storing data. Validation of data, validity and reliability of data and bias have been covered in this section. Other issues are covered in table 12.

Issue	Questions to ask yourself
Scope and size of sample	Is the size and range of your data enough to enable you to gather sufficient information to make informed recommendations and/or decisions?
Presentation of information	How will you present the data you have gathered and who will you present the information to? What organisational process should be followed when presenting information?
Ignoring measurement error	Have you calculated the measurement of error? If this is ignored, your predictions and possible recommendations will become invalid and encumber the analysis of your data.
Precision and accuracy	Have you established the difference between precision and accuracy? Is your data close to the true value – accurate? Are your data sets closer to each other rather than the true value – precise? Are they both or neither? Each of these combinations is possible and it is important to ensure that you understand the differences and that you are interpreting your data accurately.
Collection of data	What methods will you use to collect the data? Will you need to consider more than one method of collection and how will you ensure the method chosen is fit for purpose?
Performing multiple comparisons	Are you looking at a series of results from the same data? How is this affecting the measurement of error?
Causality	What causes should you consider that have impacted on the data you have gathered? The principle of cause and effect will lead you to think about whether a first process (the case) has had an impact on a second process (the effect).
Limited or unrepresentative examples	Is your sample size sufficiently large enough to gather accurate data? Have you reached the most appropriate audience to ensure the data is relevant?
Errors in methodology used	Have you checked your data for errors? What margin of error have you allowed for? Has this margin of error been communicated in the narrative of your analysis?
Interpretation problems	Are you analysing your data accurately to ensure your interpretations are truly representing the results? Are you using the best method for presenting the results, such as graphs, pie charts, narrative and so on?
Graphical representation	Are any graphs you are using easy to interpret? Have you used the most appropriate form of graph? Have you transposed the information to the graph accurately?

Table 12: Other issues relating to the analysis of data

Organisational procedures relating to data handling

There are key factors when checking that data is handled and stored safely and securely, to ensure that it is easy to retrieve and that you are operating within the law.

Be familiar with the data you hold

Establish how important the data is, what the consequences would be if you were to lose the data and how fast you need to access it. Know how long you need to keep the data, ensuring you are within organisational and GDPR guidelines. These state you should only keep personal data for the purpose which it was intended for and for as long as it is required.

Using a system that works for the organisation

It is likely that a data storage system is already installed in your organisation. It should satisfy the needs of the business rather than the other way around. Check to see what system your organisation is using. The data is likely to be stored on the premises, but there may be cloud solutions for data to be transferred easily and for remote access.

Whatever systems and procedures your organisation has in place, you should become familiar with it, and request training if required.

Maintaining confidentiality and security of data

You must be aware of the legislation and the compliance needs of the data your organisation holds. For example, for an organisation working in the hospitality industry, it is important the workforce understands the importance of the confidentiality and security of the data it holds: it is likely to include client and supplier information and other operational data.

Following data protection principles

These principles are taken from the GDPR requirements, which organisations must adhere to.

- Use data fairly and lawfully.
- Use data for limited, specifically stated purposes.
- Use data in a way that is adequate, relevant and not excessive.
- Ensure data is accurate.
- Data is kept for no longer than is necessary.
- Data is handled according to people's data protection rights.
- Data is kept safe and secure.
- Data is not transferred outside of the European Economic Area without adequate protection.

Summary

In this section you have learnt about types of data, how and when to use it and their limitations. You have also looked at how data is analysed and the importance of following organisational procedures when collecting, analysis, presenting and storing the data. This section has covered:

- business data
- qualitative and quantitative data
- the validity and reliability of data
- identified issues relating to the analysis of data to be aware of
- organisational procedures relating to data handling
- data protection principles that must be followed.

Activities

▶ **Activity 1**

What is your company's mission or vision statement?

Explain the aims and objectives of your company, their purpose and what your company wishes to achieve.

Look at your own and your team's objectives. How do these align with the overall organisational objectives?

Locate your organisational strategy. How does this align with the mission or vision statement and the organisational objectives?

Collate evidence to demonstrate how you have used KPIs to communicate activities and check your team's understanding of them. How have you given feedback to your team and measured their performance such as:

- team meetings
- notes from one-to-ones
- emails
- appraisals?

▶ **Activity 2**

Locate your company's organisational plan and/or your team plan.

How does the plan align to your organisational strategy?

What resources do you need to successfully implement the plan and how can you manage these resources?

What constraints are there, which may lead to you not being able to meet your timelines or budgets?

▶ **Activity 3**

Describe a change that you have implemented with your team.

Which change model did you use? Explain why you used this model and how it contributed to the success of the change. If you have not implemented a change, what model would you choose to use and why?

Who were your stakeholders or would be your stakeholders?

What risks did you identify that were associated with the change, or what would the likely risks be?

Collate evidence to demonstrate how you have adapted to change and identified challenges and solutions such as:

- evidence of consulting with colleagues through team meetings or emails
- witness testimony from stakeholders or your line manager, explaining how you have managed and adapted to a change
- change plan
- table identifying likely risks.

▶ Activity 4

Provide evidence to demonstrate how you organise, plan and schedule work with your team, such as:

- team rota or schedule
- budgets detailing staffing required
- details of skills required to meet organisational plan.

Provide evidence to demonstrate how you agree tasks and activities with your team such as:

- appraisals
- one-to-ones.

▶ Activity 5

Identify the data that is stored by your organisation.

What data systems are in place and how are they used?

What is the benefit to your organisation and operational management by using these systems?

Which business data and qualitative and quantitative data is used by your organisation? Explain how each is used, why it is used and the limitations of each.

Locate all policies and procedures relating to data that are in place within your organisation and identify where in each you can locate the data protection principles listed in this handbook.

Collate evidence to demonstrate how you have analysed data and presented your findings to the correct audience such as:

- presentations for key stakeholders and/or your line manager
- analysis report, including any recommendations
- tables and diagrams of your findings
- case study of your findings.

Topic consolidation

▶ Test yourself

1. An organisational strategy incorporates:

   ☐ long-term vision of goals
   ☐ daily planner
   ☐ yearly planner
   ☐ to do list.

2. The T in PESTLE analysis stands for:

   ☐ time-bound   ☐ technological
   ☐ three   ☐ technique.

3. The W in SWOT analysis stands for:

   ☐ weakness   ☐ weekly
   ☐ way forward   ☐ when.

4. The last stage in Kotter's 8-step change model is:

   ☐ make sure the team are happy
   ☐ confirm final changes with line manager
   ☐ accept the change
   ☐ anchor the change.

5. Reliability and durability of a product will be identified in which part of the performance objectives?

   ☐ cost   ☐ quality
   ☐ flexibility   ☐ speed

6. When taking remedial action, you are:

   ☐ finding a solution as quickly as possible
   ☐ keeping accurate records
   ☐ reducing waste
   ☐ recognising the impact on the environment.

7. When making changes using several smaller steps until the desired change is met, you are using:

   ☐ step change
   ☐ incremental change
   ☐ planned change
   ☐ unplanned change.

8. Qualitative data is used to:

   ☐ bench mark performance
   ☐ develop a competitive advantage
   ☐ gain descriptive information
   ☐ gain statistical information.

6

What is project management?

Project management involves managing the major stages, or milestones, of a project.

In this section you find out about the stages of the project life cycle and the common roles within project teams. You will explore the responsibilities of each of these roles and begin to consider the skills and behaviours that are required to guarantee that each of the roles is successfully fulfilled. You will also find out about the different project management tools, techniques and methods you can use to monitor and report on project progress.

The project life cycle

As a team leader or supervisor you will be required to contribute to, or even project manage, different projects. The **project life cycle** identifies the four main stages of any project and the main tasks involved; see figure 1.

It is vital that you understand the different stages and the tasks and responsibilities involved, so you can contribute effectively to the cycle. Knowing the requirements of all the stages will help you understand what and when you are expected to contribute and help you to comprehend what has happened to date in a project and the expected next steps.

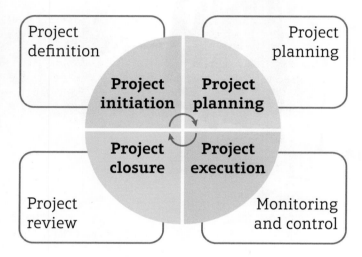

Figure 1: As a team leader, how do you plan the stages of a project?

Project initiation

This is the first stage in the project life cycle and is where the expectations and purpose of the project are agreed. At this stage you will need to clearly define the purpose of the project, identifying the reason for the project and its objectives. You will also need to define the structure of the project.

It is important to make sure your objectives are **SMART**, to ensure that everyone can see exactly what needs to be achieved and by what date. You will also need to identify **deliverables.** These are the expected outcomes of the event, ensuring that all the required resources needed throughout the project are in place and available when needed. Setting clear timescales for each stage and the tasks involved is key. Doing this enables everyone involved in the project to have a clear understanding of when they need to complete their tasks and the deadlines they must meet.

As the project manager, you will need to be aware of all the deadlines and monitor everyone's progress to ensure the project is completed on time.

Project planning

During this stage thorough plans are developed for each aspect of the project. Why each element of planning is important is shown in table 1.

Creation of project plan	Create a plan for the project to organise the different stages of the project to ensure that it will be successful.
Resource plan	Consider all the resources required for the project and plan out when and where they are needed.
Financial plan	Be aware of the project's budget and plan, what will be spent and when. Also ensure that you have the financing available at the correct time to ensure that funds are well managed and do not run out.
Quality plan	Consider and plan for the needs of your customers and how you will ensure that your project meets the correct quality standards.
Risk plan	Any project has a number of risks. These are aspects of the project that could go wrong or fail. You will need to plan for any risk to the success of the project and work to minimise these risks.
Acceptance plan	This plan will list the key success criteria of the project and include the need for approval at different stages. This will help you continue to meet the needs of your customers and ensure that the project stays on track to achieve its objectives.
Success criteria	Before you begin the project, it is vital you agree the success criteria with the people who have commissioned the project. This will include the key criteria for judging the success of the project, as well as the key deliverables that will be expected at the end of the project. The success criteria need to be SMART to ensure that everyone knows exactly what is required, by when and by whom.

Table 1: Key plans to facilitate project management

Execution

During this stage, the project will be underway and you will be responsible for ensuring that it runs to time and that all **stakeholders** are happy and informed. This involves a number of different key aspects for you to manage. At times you may review the project and make changes to your plans. You will need to consider all of them throughout the life of the project to make sure that all deliverables and success criteria are achieved.

Monitoring and controlling

By monitoring the progress of a project, you will be constantly up to date with the progress being made and ensure that you are kept informed of any key decisions made. This will help you monitor how well the project is going and control its progress.

> **Key term**
>
> **Stakeholders** – The key individuals or groups who have an interest in the project.

Skills area **S**

Skills Area 2:
Outcome Topic 2.1

Behaviours **B**

Inclusive – Open, approachable, authentic, and able to build trust with others.

Link to the standard

Knowledge Area 2:
Outcome Topic 2.1

Chain of command

This refers to how communication and messages are passed through different members of the team to ensure that everyone is kept up to date with progress and information is shared with everyone who needs it.

As a member of the project team, you must keep the project manager informed about your progress and communicate key messages to other members of your team. At times, you may also be the project manager. As part of this role, you need to communicate regularly with customers and/or senior managers to ensure that they are kept informed and agree with the progress made.

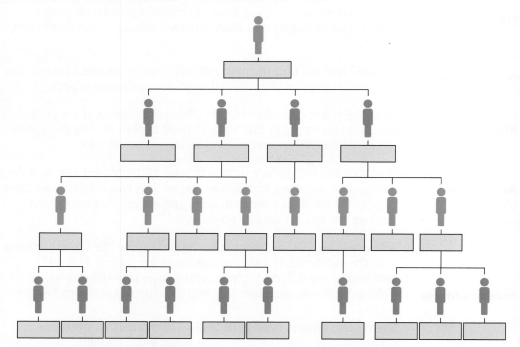

Can you describe the chain of command in your organisation?

Time management

The project will have a clear timescale and deadlines will have been set for individual stages and the project as a whole. In your role as a team leader or supervisor, you will play an important part in ensuring that the team works to the deadlines set and that their time is managed well to ensure that they achieve their individual objectives in the timescale provided.

Cost management

Ensure that, throughout the project life cycle, costs and budgets are managed. Regularly review the budgets set and ensure that spending does not exceed the amount allocated. If spending in one area of the project is too high, you will need to look at cutting costs elsewhere to ensure that the overall budget is met. You will find further information about managing costs and budgets in Section 8.

Quality management

You will also need to manage the quality of the project, making sure that customer expectations are met and quality standards are maintained. You will need to report and act upon any issues about quality during the project life cycle.

Change management

At times, changes may be required during the project that reflect changes in priority within the organisation or where issues with initial plans have been identified. This needs careful management and you will need to review what needs changing before developing strategies to make the changes needed. You will also need to communicate changes to the customer or team to ensure that they are happy with them and understand why they are necessary. You may find some resistance to the changes and therefore you will need to convince those with concerns that the changes are required and are in the best interest of the project.

Risk management

In the initial stages of the project you will have identified risks to the project. Once you have identified the potential risks, you will need to work with your team to put strategies in place to avoid them. It is important that throughout the life of the project you regularly check identified risks to ensure the project's successful completion.

Issue management

Not all risks can be avoided and sometimes they develop into issues that block the project's deliverables being achieved. Additionally, unexpected issues arise and will need addressing. Encourage your team to look for and report any issues so that you can work together to resolve any issues and get the project back on track.

Acceptance management

If changes are made, inform the customer or the person who commissioned the project. Ensure that they agree to any changes being made. You will need to amend the plan with the changes made and get sign off from the project commissioner. This will help avoid disagreement or disappointment at the end of the project.

Communication management

A vital aspect of ensuring that the project is successful is communicating with everyone involved throughout its duration. You will need to use the skills that you have explored in *Chapter 3 Building relations* in the *Communication* section, to help you communicate with your team and others involved in the project to ensure that everyone is informed of the progress made.

Closure and evaluation

As the project comes to completion, it will need to be closed effectively. Review the objectives of the project and success criteria to judge how effective the project has been.

By evaluating the project and gathering feedback from everyone involved on the effectiveness of the project, you will be able to identify the aspects of the project that have gone well and those that haven't. From this you can reflect on aspects that could be improved in future projects. By examining the lessons learned you can avoid any issues in future projects and build on any successes.

Summary

This section was about the project life cycle and the major milestones for a project.
- The common role and responsibilities of project teams.

Common roles and responsibilities within project teams

Skills area **S**

Skills Area 2:
Outcome Topic 2.1

Behaviours **B**

Takes responsibility –
Drive to achieve in all
aspects of work.

**Link to the
standard** 🔗

Knowledge Area 2:
Outcome Topic 2.1

There are a number of common roles and responsibilities within project teams;
see figure 2. At different times you will undertake each of these roles and will
need to understand them to ensure that you fulfil the role.

It is important to understand each role so that you know who is responsible for doing
what when completing projects, as show in table 2.

| Project manager | Project sponsor | Project board | Senior consultant | Project team member | Project administrator/coordinator |

Figure 2: Which role do you take in your organisation?

Role	Responsibility
Project manager	A project manager is responsible for managing the overall project and developing the definition and objectives of the project. They are responsible for ensuring the project is delivered on time, managing the budget, ensuring the project does not overspend and meeting quality standards. The project manager is also responsible for managing the relationships between all those contributing to the project.
Project sponsor	The project sponsor commissions others to deliver the project and will define the project to the project manager. They will outline the requirements of the project and set the key objectives. A project sponsor expects updates and reviews of the projects at regular intervals.
Project board	The project board oversees the progress of the project and will react to strategic problems, developing solutions to the problems.
Senior consultant	The senior consultant manages the input from suppliers, ensuring that sufficient resources are provided in a timely manner.
Project team members	The project team members are the staff who actively work on a project to ensure that it is successful. They will each contribute to different aspects of the project, dependent on the type of project being undertaken.
Project administrator/coordinator	The project administrator/coordinator is responsible for managing and updating the project plan and provides administrative support to the whole team to assist them in successfully completing the project.

Table 2: Project roles and responsibilities

Project management tools and techniques

While working on, or managing, a project you will use a number of different tools and techniques to ensure that the project is successful. Furthermore, you will develop methods to monitor and report on project progress to different stakeholders of the project.

Project management key tools and documents

There are a number of key tools and documents that are used in project management, with which you will need to be familiar in your role as team leader or supervisor.

Business case/project plan

A business case outlines all the details of the planned project and is used to help decide whether the project is worthwhile. It brings together information on the key risks, costs, benefits and drawbacks of a project, not only at the current time but also for the future. This can then be combined with the project plan to be presented to those commissioning the project. It is therefore important that you as the team leader or supervisor are fully aware of the requirements of the business case and what to include if you are required to develop one for a project.

Checklists/activity lists

Checklists or activity lists used throughout the life of the project include a list of tasks and activities that need to be completed at the different stages of the project. Using a format like this allows you to check regularly that everything that needs to be done has been completed.

Link to the standard

Knowledge Area 2: Outcome Topic 2.2

Skills area

Skills Area 2: Outcome Topic 2.1

Skills Area 2: Outcome Topic 2.2

Behaviours

Agile – Positive and adaptable, responds well to feedback and need to change.

How can you improve the way you keep track of tasks?

Charting analysis

You may also need to use chart analysis to plot the progress of the project. Charts can be useful in displaying a range of different information in one format and can be used to plan the project. There are a number of different charts that can be used.

Gantt charts

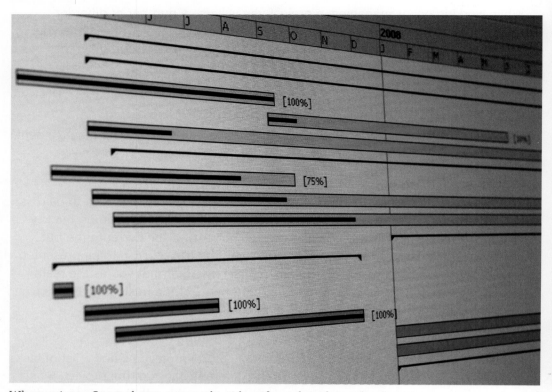

When using a Gantt chart, you need to identify each task involved

Gantt charts can be used to plan projects. They include the tasks involved, their order and the timescales, including when and how long each task will take and who is responsible for each task. You should also highlight any issues that the project may face.

You will easily see when each task is due to start and when it will end, so you can check on the progress made. It is easy to amend the timescale and order of tasks to help you manage the progress of the project.

The flowchart shown in figure 3 will help you in creating a Gantt chart. You can also use a range of software to help you to create your Gantt chart.

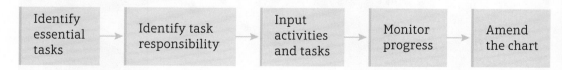

Figure 3: These steps help to create a thorough plan

Load charts

A load chart is one that shows the amount of work that is still required on a project. It is usually used in manufacturing projects and works in a similar manner to a Gantt chart.

Project management tools and techniques

Critical paths

Using **critical path analysis** helps to organise, plan and monitor the progress of a project. Identifying the critical path, will show you the best, most efficient and fastest process to use, to complete the project.

Risk management logs

These include all the risks and hazards involved in a project. Once the risks have been identified, then strategies and actions to avoid the risks can be developed and added to the log. This may help you in planning and monitoring the project and avoid any risks that prevent the project being successful.

Dependencies

Dependencies in a project are relationships between two or more activities/tasks. It may be that one task/activity must be completed before another can begin or tasks/activities need to be completed together to be successful. You will need to identify these dependencies as they could affect the progress of the project and may be being undertaken by different team members.

Responsibilities

It is important to be aware of your responsibilities and those of your team members during the project. Review the responsibilities of the team at different stages of the project and implement any different or extra responsibilities across the team as needed.

Cost-benefit analysis

When making decisions during a project, you may find cost-benefit analysis useful. This is where you consider the positive aspects (benefits) of the actions/project/idea and the negative aspects (costs). List them all to help you make the correct decision.

Techniques and methods used in project monitoring

Using these techniques and methods can help you in the following ways.

- **Allows for the monitoring of project team.** Throughout the life of the project, you will need to monitor the project team to make sure that the quality of work is of the standard expected and they are meeting deadlines.

- **Allows informed decisions to be made.** The techniques outlined will also help you make the necessary decisions, considering all the information available.

- **Allows suggestions/adjustments to plan.** You can also use them to find suggestions to improve the project or reflect and adjust your plans.

- **Steer the team in the right direction.** At times you need to focus your team in the correct direction. Use the project management techniques outlined here to help you do this.

- **Evaluate the project.** Reflect upon and evaluate the project. Look at the successes of the project and where it went wrong.

Key term

Critical path analysis – Involves analysing the different stages of a project to find the shortest sequence of stages to completing the project – the 'critical path'.

Link to the standard

Knowledge Area 2: Outcome Topic 2.2

Skills area

Skills Area 2: Outcome Topic 2.2

Behaviours

Agile – Is creative, innovative and enterprising when seeking solution to business needs.

- **Lessons learned to inform future projects.** Once you have evaluated the project, you can then identify the lessons you have learned to help you in future projects, helping to avoid the mistakes that you have made in other projects.

Management of project progress

There are a number of different skills and functions involved in managing the progress of the project. Ensure that you know how to keep the project on schedule. Some of the following methods may help you to do so.

- **Planning and scheduling** We have already identified the plans that need to be put in place before a project is started earlier in this section. You will need to plan out the project and ensure that sufficient time is scheduled for each stage to ensure that you complete the project by the deadline.

- **Objectives** It is important to review these objectives throughout the life of the project, considering how far the objectives are being met and if they need to be revised.

- **Schedules** At times during the project, the timescale and schedule initially established may not be realistic. Review the schedule for the project and make ongoing changes to ensure that the project is completed on time.

- **Sequencing** You may also need to look at the sequencing of the different stages of the project. Reflect on and change the order of the stages in the project or adapt the timescale allowed for each stage in the sequence.

- **Activities and work breakdown** When managing a project, ensure that you include all the activities required to complete the project and allocate activities to different team members. Consider the breakdown of work for each individual and reassess this at different times if it seems that some have too much work and others too little.

A number of methods can help you keep your project and your tasks on track

Critical path analysis You could use critical path analysis to help you work out how long the project should take and decide on the shortest path of stages involved to complete the project.

- **Basic budgeting** Manage the project's budget and ensure that you do not spend more than you have been allocated.

- **Estimating skills** When deciding on the costs involved in a project or the timescale of an individual stage of the project, you will need to create estimates using estimating skills. Your estimates will be based on research you should do on similar projects, costs or timescales to make them as accurate as they can be.

- **Direct and indirect costs** When managing the project be aware of the **direct** and **indirect** costs of the project.

- **Cash flow modelling** This involves listing all the inflows (money coming into the business) and outflows (money going out of the business) for the project. The inflows and outflows are then adapted and changed to provide different models or scenarios to allow you to look at different options and identify where contingency planning is needed.

- **Contingency planning** During the life of a project, things may change that you may or may not have predicted. This is when you need to use contingency planning to respond to changes. You will need to be flexible and adapt your approach to the project to ensure that it is successful.

Key terms

Direct costs – Those costs that can be directly attributed to the production process such as the cost of raw materials or stock.

Indirect costs – Costs that cannot be attributed directly to the production process such as administration or marketing.

Cash flow – The money coming into and going out of the business.

Link to the standard

Knowledge Area 2: Outcome Topic 2.2

Skills area

Skills Area 2: Outcome Topic 2.2

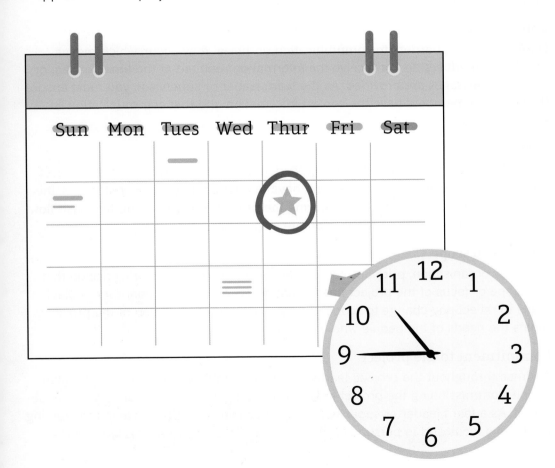

How do you manage time in a project?

Identifying problems related to project progress

As we have discussed throughout this section, sometimes projects do not run to plan and things may go wrong. These problems need to be identified and strategies put in place to get the project back on track. There are several common issues that can affect the success of a project.

Risk assessment

The risk assessment may not have identified key risks and things that can go wrong or it may not have identified the correct level of severity. You will need to be prepared to review the risk assessment of the project throughout its life cycle.

Time/not meeting deadlines

Although you will have researched how long different activities/stages in the project should take, sometimes these take longer than expected and the project may be at risk of not meeting deadlines. You will need to look at how you can amend the workloads of staff and adapt timescales to help resolve this.

Resources

While you will have identified the resources required to complete the project at the planning stage, you may not have fully appreciated how many resources are required. Alternatively, additional resources may have been identified during the project. Review the number and availability of resources at regular intervals to ensure they are sufficient to complete the project.

Communication

During a project, barriers to communication or 'noise' may occur, which means that team members do not receive the information required at the time needed, or incorrect messages are provided. As the team leader or supervisor, you must ensure that all team members have the correct information and that communication is effective and timely.

Costings

You will have used cash flow modelling to identify the costs involved in the project. Sometimes, however, the estimates you have developed may not be realistic or the costs of key resources may change during the project. Review and update cash flow models to ensure that they are as accurate as possible.

Changes to scope

In a busy organisation, priorities can change or the project board may decide that the scope or focus of the project has to change. Be prepared to adapt the project plans to reflect any change to scope, to ensure that the completion of the project meets the needs of the people who have commissioned it.

Commitment to the project

At times throughout the project, teams can lose commitment to the project. The people commissioning the project may doubt the team's ability or drive to continue with it. As a team leader or supervisor, you will play an important role in maintaining the team's focus and in persuading those involved that the project is worthwhile.

Summary

In this section you have learned about project management, the project life cycle and key project milestones. This section has covered:

- techniques and methods used to monitor and report on project progress
- methods used to identify problems related to project progress.

Activities

▶ Activity 1

Think about a project you are currently working on. Use the project life cycle to help you plan out the project, considering each of the stages and what you will need to do at each stage.

▶ Activity 2

Identify all the people involved in a recent project you have been involved with.

Using a table like table 3, make a list of each person's roles and responsibilities.

Include specific examples of the tasks and activities they undertook. You may want to reflect on how well they carried out their responsibilities.

Individual	Role	Responsibilities	Tasks/activities

Table 3: Example table to list people's roles and responsibilities

▶ Activity 3

Consider all the different project management tools that have been explored in this section. For each one, make notes about how you can could use them within your role when contributing to different projects at work.

If you have used any of the tools, also make a note of how well you have used them and what you might need to improve upon.

▶ Activity 4

Reflect on a project you have managed or contributed to.

- What techniques did you use to ensure the progress of the project?
- What problems did you face? Did you overcome them?
- What could you have done differently to improve the performance of the project?

Topic consolidation

▶ Test yourself

1. What is the correct order of the project life cycle?

    ☐ project initiation, project planning, project review, monitoring and control
    ☐ project planning, project initiation, project review, monitoring and control
    ☐ project planning, project initiation, monitoring and control, project review
    ☐ project planning, project review, project initiation, monitoring and control

2. How happy and confident were you in your most recent project role:

    ☐ very happy and confident
    ☐ somewhat happy and confident
    ☐ unhappy and not at all confident
    ☐ extremely unhappy and not at all confident

3. When leading a project, were you:

    ☐ friendly
    ☐ assertive
    ☐ approachable
    ☐ relaxed?

4. When planning a project, did you:

    ☐ consider the needs of the client
    ☐ decide straight away what you were going to do
    ☐ delegate all the planning to other people
    ☐ agree the success criteria in advance?

5. Consider a time when you were managing a project:

    ☐ Did you stick to the initial plan no matter what?
    ☐ Were you flexible and change things regularly?
    ☐ Did you leave everyone alone to do their own jobs?
    ☐ Did you check all changes with the project board?

6. When reviewing the success of the project, were you:

    ☐ positive and willing to respond well to feedback
    ☐ willing to seek the views of others
    ☐ open and honest
    ☐ able to operate within organisational values?

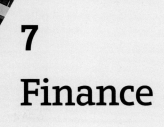

7

Finance

What is organisational governance and compliance?

Every organisation has policies, processes and procedures in place to ensure that they comply with government requirements. There are a range of different requirements and legislations, produced by external agencies which work for the government. Organisations have to comply with these. An organisation will also have its own compliance requirements. You will explore these requirements and the policies, processes and procedures put in place by the organisation to ensure that you work within their expectations. You will also learn about:

- the purpose of business accounting
- types, uses, management and limitations of budgets
- basic financial terminology
- the identification and management of costs within the workplace.

Compliance requirements

Your organisation must ensure that it follows a number of different requirements on a day to day basis. Some of these will be set by external agencies and some will be set by the organisation itself.

External requirements

There are a number of external requirements set by the government that your organisation has to comply with.

Preparing confirmation statements and company accounts for Companies House

Companies House is the government agency responsible for registering companies in the UK. As a registered company, your organisation will have to prepare and publish confirmation statements each year. The confirmation statement contains details of the company which must be updated each year to confirm that the information is still correct.

Your company will also have to produce company accounts and send them to Companies House. These accounts are the documents that record all the financial transactions of the company during the year.

Notifying Companies House about changes to company details

In addition to producing confirmation statements, your company must inform Companies House of any changes in its company details during the year, if changes occur before their submission of their confirmation statement.

Behaviours

Professionalism – Open and honest.

Link to the standard

Knowledge Area 2: Outcome Topic 3.1

Skills area

Skills Area 2: Outcome Topic 3.1.

Paying corporation tax

As a registered company, your organisation must pay **corporation tax**. You must pay this tax as a limited company, as a UK branch or office of a foreign company and as a club, cooperative or other unincorporated association, such as a sports club.

Filing tax returns and annual accounts with HMRC

To help calculate the level of tax your organisation has to pay, it must file tax returns with Her Majesty's Revenues and Customs (HMRC). This is the government agency responsible for collecting tax. In order to ensure that the right level of tax is paid, a company should submit a copy of its annual accounts to HMRC.

Internal requirements

There are also internal requirements your organisation must comply with.

Tracking income and expenditure

To help your organisation manage its finances and ensure there are no errors in its annual accounts, it must track **income** and **expenditure**. This is the money that comes into the organisation and the money that goes out.

If you are responsible for either spending the organisation's money or collecting payments, you must make sure you follow the organisation's policies and procedures to ensure that you are tracking income and expenditure effectively and no mistakes are made.

Setting up and maintaining organisational records to meet requirements of governance and compliance

The organisation will also need to set up systems to produce company accounts and to keep these up to date. These accounts will be used by the organisation internally, but also form the basis of the annual accounts required by Companies House and HMRC. It must keep records of any changes to company details, such as changes in the company directors, to ensure that this information is maintained and shared with Companies House.

Assisting with audits to provide stakeholder assurance that financial statements are accurate

Each registered company will use third party companies to check that the records and financial documentation produced is accurate. This is to ensure that all stakeholders can be assured that the financial statements produced are accurate and true. This is vital to ensure **stakeholder** trust in the organisation.

Key terms

Corporation tax – Tax on a company's profits.

Income – Money that is generated, or coming into the organisation.

Expenditure – Money spent, or going out of the organisation.

Governance – The policies, processes and procedures that exist to satisfy the requirements of the government and statutory compliance requirements.

Compliance – Adherence to laws, policies and procedures.

Stakeholders – Individuals or groups that have an interest in the organisation.

Purpose of business accounting

Behaviours

Agile – Flexible to meet the needs of the organisation.

Link to the standard

Knowledge Area 2: Outcome Topic 3.1

Skills area

Skills Area 2: Outcome Topic 3.1.

Business accounting is the recording, interpreting and presentation of financial information. This is the way the organisation keeps track of its finances. There are a number of purposes of business accounting.

Recording transactions

Business accounting allows organisations to record transactions. This means that your organisation can record all the income and expenditure on an ongoing basis, helping to feed information into annual accounts and other financial documentation required at the end of each year. In your role as a team leader or supervisor, you should ensure that you and your team work within the processes and procedures in place to support this.

Monitoring activity

Monitoring how the organisation is working and the activities it undertakes, means it can identify trends in income and expenditure and any changes. Furthermore, it can identify any areas for concern and put strategies in place to correct them. You may be asked to report on the financial performance of your team to help provide information towards this.

Control management of the business

Business accounting also helps in the planning, monitoring and control of the organisation. It will help the organisation plan its finances and future operations by considering its past activity and deciding on what the business can afford to do in future. It also allows your organisation to monitor the performance of business and how well it is doing in line with its budgets. If the organisation is not keeping within budget, then the expenditure can be identified, reviewed and controlled.

Measurement of financial performance

Business accounting can also be used to measure the financial performance of a business, and judge how well the organisation is performing. A number of different ways you can measure the financial performance of the organisation are outlined below.

- **Gross profit** This takes the money brought in from sales (sales revenue) and deducts the cost of the stock bought or the raw materials bought to make the product (direct costs). This helps the organisation decide if individual products are going to be profitable.

- **Net profit** This takes account of all the other costs an organisation needs to pay for. Once the direct costs have been deducted from sales revenue to calculate gross profit, all the other costs are then deducted. These costs are called expenses. Once they have been deducted, this results in net profit. This shows the overall profitability of an organisation.

- **Value owed to the business** This is money that the business is owed from customers, etc. Your organisation must stay informed and ensure that this money is collected.

- **Value owed by the business** This is money the business owes to other businesses and banks. Your organisation must keep a record of how much it owes, when it needs to be repaid and the rate of interest that is being charged. Interest is a charge, which is a percentage of the money owed.

Auditing

Financial auditing is the process of examining financial records to establish if they are correct and in accordance with any regulations and laws. External auditors work outside an organisation to examine financial records and prepare and provide an independent opinion on these records. By law, all public companies must have their financial statements externally audited.

Auditors ensure financial statements are accurate

Types, uses, management and limitations of budgets

Budgeting is important to all businesses. This involves planning how much money will come into the business and how much will go out. You must work within a **budget** when undertaking projects and during the day to day running of the organisation. Understanding the different types of budgets, how to manage a budget and their limitations will help in your team leader or supervisor role.

Types of budgets

There are a number of different budgets that you will need to work with and manage.

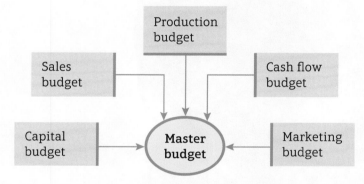

Figure 1: Identify how your budgetary responsibility feeds into the master budget in your organisation

Master budget

The master budget is the overall budget, including all other budgets within the organisation; see figure 1. This will be broken into different weeks and months, as well as the year. A senior member of staff and/or the finance department will usually be responsible for this budget. In your role, you may have responsibility for one of the budgets that are included within it.

Capital budget

The capital budget focuses on all the organisation's **fixed assets**. These are items the organisation owns that will last for a long period of time, such as machinery and vehicles. The capital budget looks at how long the assets will last, how they depreciate in value and when they will need replacing. It will also include any planned expenditure on new assets, estimating the return the company will get on the investment. This decides whether the investment is worthwhile or not.

Sales budget

The sales budget focuses on money coming into the business or income. The organisation will set a sales budget for itself overall, teams and individuals. This is the predicted level of sales that should be made in a period of time. It is likely that in your role as a team leader or supervisor, you will be responsible for working towards a sales budget, focusing on your team's target as well as your own.

Production budget

A production budget focuses on how many different products need to be made in a certain period of time. It will look at the stock already available, the predicted number of sales and how many products need to be made or bought to ensure that there is enough stock to fulfil orders. You may have to work with a production budget, ensuring that you and your team meet the targets set to help the organisation meet its overall master budget.

Cash flow budget

A **cash flow** budget estimates all the income and expenditure of the organisation during a certain period of time. This usually takes the form of a cash flow forecast. You may need to contribute estimates of costs and sales to be included in the organisation's cash flow budget.

Marketing budget

A marketing budget focuses on the costs required to promote the organisation's products. It includes all the promotional costs as well as the costs of staff required to complete this activity. **Marketing** is the activity used by the organisation to tell people about its products and try and convince them to buy them. You may have to manage a marketing budget in your role, especially when managing projects.

> **Key terms**
>
> **Cash flow** – The flow of money into and out of the organisation.
>
> **Marketing** – The activity of buying, selling, distributing and promoting products.

Sales may come from high street consumers or business to business service providers.

Uses of budgets

> You should understand how to use budgets in your role as a team leader or supervisor.

Budgets are used to control income and expenditure, and to help the organisation ensure that it has enough money coming in to cover all the costs that it needs to pay for, leaving over some profit. Table 1 gives examples of how budgets are used to control and support other elements of an organisation.

Establish numerical priorities and targets	Budgets are used to help to determine what is important and needs to be achieved. They are also used to set targets for individuals and teams.
Provide direction and coordination	Budgets help to decide on what needs doing and what direction the organisation, teams or individuals need to take to achieve objectives. In addition, the master budget will help make everyone aware of what each individual department must do to meet the overall budget. It helps coordinate everyone's efforts to achieve this.
Assign responsibilities	Responsibilities for achieving targets can also be identified through the use of budgeting as they clearly lay out what needs to be achieved.
Improve efficiency	By setting and managing budgets, the organisation can minimise costs and maximise production and sales. This can help the organisation be more efficient and boost profitability.
Monitor performance	By managing budgets and reviewing targets within them, the organisation can monitor and evaluate its performance. It can also monitor the performance of teams and individuals by reviewing their contribution to achieving the overall budgets.
Inform management decisions	Budgets can also help inform future management decisions. If budgets are not met, this may indicate that changes need to be made or a change in direction is required. Therefore, they provide effective evidence to support decisions.
Plan future activities	Budgets can be used to plan future activities by reviewing the performance towards targets and analysing what has, and has not, been successful in the past.
Support innovation	Budgeting can help identify funds for innovation and research and development. The capital budget also analyses future investment plans and decides whether they are likely to be successful or not.
Fund training	Finally, in a similar manner, budgeting can effectively free up money to fund training schemes to ensure that staff are developed and have the skills that the organisation requires.

Table 1: How are budgets used in the organisation where you work?

How to manage a budget

You must learn how to manage a budget to help you in your role of team leader or supervisor. You will have some experience of managing a budget on a day to day basis through managing your own finances. You will have monitored how much money you have coming in and how much you need to spend, and then make decisions about what you are going to buy or not. Managing a budget involves similar skills and activities.

Identifying priorities and timescales

In managing a budget, you should prioritise what is necessary and what isn't required, and make decisions about what to purchase or not. You ought to prioritise different tasks and activities to ensure that budgets are met in the required timescale.

Negotiating and agreeing financial resources

You should consider the appropriateness of the budget set, or estimate how much is required and negotiate this with your line manager or finance department.

Accurate recording of income and expenditure

You must accurately record income and expenditure, keeping records up to date to ensure that you can monitor performance towards meeting the budgets set. You will need to produce accounts to keep these records.

Monitoring income and expenditure against planned activity

Once you have recorded income and expenditure, you should monitor this income and expenditure against planned activity. It is not sufficient to review past income and expenditure, as you need to also consider what is planned in future to ensure there is no overspend or income is lower than forecast.

Taking corrective actions if budgets are not met

If budgets are not met, you should find solutions and take corrective actions to ensure that budgets are met within the timescale. It is crucial that you review progress towards budgets constantly to give yourself time to plan and implement corrective action.

Investigating unaccounted variances

A variance occurs where the actual figure achieved is different to the budget set. If you do not achieve the budget, you will be expected to account for the variance. If you do not know why the budget has not been met, you should investigate and report back to your line manager or finance department, providing reasons for the variance.

Updating budgets

At times, a budget may be unrealistic and either won't be achieved or needs increasing as it has already been exceeded. In this instance, you should review budgets and renegotiate them and update them to ensure that you are working towards the correct target.

Dealing with unforeseen internal and external situations and changes

You will need to reflect on unforeseen internal and external situations, and where there is a risk of not meeting the budget. You may need to take corrective actions or update the budget accordingly.

Negotiating revisions to budgets

At times you will have to negotiate revisions to budgets, to ensure that you and your team have a fair chance of achieving them. You should use some of the negotiation techniques and skills in Section 3 to help you negotiate and agree the level of financial resources and the budget set.

What factors would influence budget negotiation in your role?

Reporting and communicating changes

When you make any changes to your budget, it is important to report them to anyone else they affect. This may be your team or someone else in the organisation. It is vital that you communicate any changes to the person who manages the master budget or other budgets it feeds into.

Limitations of budgets

While budgets are very useful in helping an organisation manage its finances, they do have their limitations.

Can lead to inflexibility in decision-making
Setting rigid budgets can lead to inflexibility in decision-making. Sometimes organisations can become too focused on meeting budgets and can make decisions solely based on them. This can mean they are unlikely to review decisions or change them.

Need to be changed as circumstances change
Budgets sometimes need to change and you should be aware of this, reflecting on changes in circumstances and adapting budgets to reflect them. Otherwise, budgets become less useful and may not help the organisation to achieve its objectives.

Can result in short-term decisions rather than long-term decisions
If an organisation, team or individual focuses too much on achieving weekly and monthly budgets, it can start to make decisions focused on the short-term achievement of the budget. They may not consider the long-term implications of these decisions. For example even though a decision may mean exceeding the budget in the short-term, it may prevent problems in the long-term. Therefore, consider both the short-term and long-term together in making decisions.

Can create some behavioural challenges in a business
Setting budgets can be a useful motivation tool (see Section 2). While focusing on a target can motivate people to work, it can also make people competitive and this may have a detrimental effect on relationships within teams. People can also become too focused on working within a budget, not realising that other aspects of their role may be important too.

Behaviours B

Takes responsibility – Determination when managing difficult situations.

Link to the standard

Knowledge Area 2: Outcome Topic 3.1

Skills area S

Skills Area 2: Outcome Topic 3.1

Financial terminology

There are a number of financial terms that you may come across when working as a team leader or supervisor. Table 2 is a list of useful terms you will encounter when dealing with finance at work.

Terms	Definition/explanation
Income	Money that flows into the organisation, including money made from sales.
Expenditure	Money that flows out of the organisation. This includes the costs of raw materials and stock, expenses and repayments of loans, etc.
Transaction	The exchange of money when something is bought or sold.
Cash flow	The flow of money in and out of the organisation.
Accounts	A record of financial transactions that have taken place in an organisation.
Gross profit	The money made from selling products or services after the cost of making them or buying them has been paid.
Net profit	The profit made after all costs and expenses have been paid from the money brought in from sales.
Capital	The money or assets the organisation holds.
Debtors	These are the people or organisations that owe the organisation money.
Creditors	These are the people or organisations the organisation owes money to.
Turnover	This is the money made from sales during a certain time period.
Profit and loss account	This is a financial document that records the financial transactions made and calculates the different forms of profit. This may be also called an income statement.
Balance sheet	This is a financial document that records the amount of money the organisation owns and the money it owes. It also includes how the organisation has been funded during a period of time. This is also called a statement of financial position.
Fixed costs	These are costs that do not vary over output levels, such as rent.
Variable costs	These are costs that vary over output levels, such as wages.

Break-even point	This is the level of output where no level of profit or loss is made. The organisation will just cover all its costs, but no money will be left over.
Tax	This is a compulsory contribution of money paid to the government.
VAT	This is value added tax, which is tax paid on goods and services.
Asset	An item of value that an organisation owns.
Depreciation	This is the fall in the value of an asset over time.
Investment	This involves investing money into the organisation to make more profit.
Accruals	These are expenses or money that has been earned but not yet received. They are recorded in the financial account.
Stock	These are the organisation's finished products that are available to be sold.
Liabilities	These are debts that are due to be paid, including items such as money owed to creditors and loans to be repaid.

Table 2: Financial terms

Managing cost in the workplace

Behaviours

Professional – Open and honest.

Link to the standard

Knowledge Area 2:
Outcome Topic 3.1

Skills area

Skills Area 2:
Outcome Topic 3.1.

Management of costs is vital to the success of an organisation. If costs increase, then the organisation may not make a profit without raising prices or cutting costs elsewhere.

Categories of cost

There are a number of categories of cost that you need to identify and understand. Table 3 outlines the source and impact of each.

Material costs	Materials are the things used to produce your organisation's products or services. You should control and monitor these to maximise the organisation's profit.
Labour costs	Labour is the worker hours used in the organisation. Wages can be a large proportion of the overall costs of the organisation. In your role, you must consider the number of hours your team are working, how much that costs overall and keep this is line with budgets.
Overhead costs	Overheads are the expenses the organisation has to pay for. They are the other costs a business has to pay above the costs of sales.
Fixed costs	Fixed costs do not fluctuate over output levels. These are items such as mortgage payments, rent or salaries.
Variable costs	These are items you need to pay for per item. For example, wages, utility bills (electricity, gas or water bills).
Semi-variable costs	Semi-variable costs are a combination of fixed and variable costs. Some items such as a telephone or internet connection have a fixed cost, the cost of the service and then a cost for usage. This needs consideration, as often people forget about the cost of usage and bills can be higher than expected.
Direct costs	Direct costs are the costs that can be directly attributed to the production process, such as the cost of stock or materials.
Indirect costs	These are expenses, for everything other than the direct costs. They need monitoring to avoid them escalating and eating into the organisation's profit.
Apportioned costs	Apportioned costs are those that are allocated or associated with a certain department, production process or project. You should be aware of the costs apportioned to your team or department and manage them appropriately.

Table 3: The sources and impacts of different types of cost

Controlling material costs

It is also very important to control the costs of materials. Here are some examples of methods of controlling material cost that you can use, or can be used by your organisation.

Ordering methods and systems

You will need to think about the best system or method to order the items you need to help control the cost. Ordering too much can mean waste, which costs the organisation money. However, ordering too little may mean you don't have enough and have to order more items. Overall this might cost more because bulk orders often attract greater discounts and cost less per item.

Issuing goods/resources

Issuing goods/resources to the team only when they are needed, rather than making them readily available, can help you control how much is used.

Minimum stock levels

Keeping stock levels to a minimum will limit wastage and require less storage space. Think about how much of a material you are likely to use and only order this amount.

Safety and security of storage

Ensuring that materials are stored safely will stop them being damaged and remain in good condition. You will also need to consider the security of any storage facility to ensure that materials are secure.

Performance indicators

It is important to be aware of the performance indicators that will help you decide on the level of materials that are required and how effectively they are used. These include the sales mix, which measures the proportion of the organisation's products sold. It looks at each individual product and calculates what proportion of overall sales each product accounts for.

Average spend is another performance indicator. This calculates how much each different type of customer spends on average. This can help inform how many of these products you need to hold in stock or the amount of materials you need to make them.

Documentation

You will also need to understand the uses of different documentation used in the management of stock and materials; see figure 2.

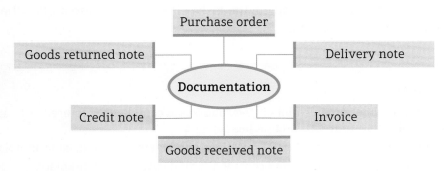

Figure 2: Which of these documents do you use in your role?

Behaviours

Agile – Flexible to the needs of the organisation.

Link to the standard

Knowledge Area 2: Outcome Topic 3.1

Skills area

Skills Area 2: Outcome Topic 3.1.

Identify the busy and quiet periods of work for your team. What are the reasons for this?

Purchase order This document is used to itemise the materials that are ordered from a supplier when the order is placed.

Delivery note The delivery note is provided when materials are delivered and is signed by the person receiving them.

Invoice This is sent to the buyer, itemising the quantities and cost of all items that have been purchased. The overall amount due is also included.

Goods received note This is an internal document that checks that all the items ordered have been received in a delivery. It provides evidence against the delivery note to prove what has been provided.

Credit note A credit note is offered when goods are returned as a form of refund. The value of the refund is included in the credit note for the customer to use for future purchases with the issuing supplier.

Goods returned note This document is sent with goods that are returned to a supplier, itemising the goods returned and the reasons for it.

Controlling labour costs

Labour is one of the largest costs an organisation has and, therefore, anything you can do to control labour costs, will help your organisation minimise their overall costs and maximise profits.

Efficient scheduling

Efficiently scheduling work can help control labour costs. Consider when there is greatest demand in the organisation and when the busiest times are. Schedule more staff to work during busy periods and less during quieter times.

You should think in advance about the labour needs of your team and organise rotas to allow for this. There will be peaks and troughs in business during the year and you should reflect this in your labour forecasts.

Maximising workforce effectiveness

Make sure that your team work efficiently and maximise workforce effectiveness at all times. Planning work tasks in the correct order and in the most efficient way possible will help. Additionally, matching the right people, with the right skills, to the right tasks will improve the effectiveness of the team.

You can also set and track efficiency goals, to encourage your team to work hard and resourcefully. Monitoring how staff work, their progress on tasks, keeping them on task and motivating them to complete the tasks effectively can also reduce the time they take and lower the labour costs.

Summary

This section was about organisational governance and compliance requirements, and the purpose of accounting. This section has covered:
- the types, uses, management and limitations of budgets and financial terminology
- the different ways to manage and control different costs in the workplace.

Activities

▶ **Activity 1**

Investigate how your organisation handles different compliance requirements.

- Who is responsible for filing tax returns and confirmation statements?
- What company account documentation does your organisation produce and publish?
- What internal and external audits does the organisation organise?

▶ **Activity 2**

Think about a budget you or your organisation use.

- What type of budget is it?
- How does it link to other budgets held by others in the organisation?
- How do you manage the budget?
- What works well and what doesn't?
- How could you handle it differently?
- What problems are there with using budgets in your role?

▶ **Activity 3**

Make a list of all the financial terminology you use in your role. Do you understand what all the words mean? Use the information provided in table 2 to help you form your own definitions for the different words you use.

▶ **Activity 4**

Think about how you manage and control costs in the workplace. How can you control material costs and labour costs in your role? List ideas for reducing/controlling costs in your department.

Topic consolidation

▶ Test yourself

1. Fixed costs:

   ☐ do not fluctuate over output levels
   ☐ do fluctuate over output levels
   ☐ are items you need to pay for per item
   ☐ are the things used to produce your organisation's products or services.

2. Direct costs:

   ☐ are the expenses the organisation has to pay for
   ☐ can be directly attributed to the production process, such as the cost of stock or materials
   ☐ are items you need to pay for per item
   ☐ are a combination of fixed and variable costs.

3. When working with finances and financial documentation, how confident do you feel?

   ☐ I am always confident.
   ☐ Sometimes I feel confident.
   ☐ I rarely feel confident.
   ☐ I never feel confident.

4. Think of a time when you had to work with a budget. Did you:

   ☐ review the budget at the end of the period
   ☐ stick to the original budget no matter what
   ☐ update the budget regularly
   ☐ demand that the budget be changed?

5. When you have managed a budget do you:

   ☐ show integrity
   ☐ act professionally
   ☐ pay attention to detail
   ☐ operate within organisational values?

6. In your role, when managing costs, do you:

   ☐ ensure that you and your team only use what materials are necessary
   ☐ allow staff to use as many materials as required
   ☐ allow your team to complete the tasks they enjoy and want to do
   ☐ consider the labour needs of the team and schedule staff accordingly?

8
Self-awareness

Self-awareness is the skill of understanding yourself; your strengths and limitations. This is a difficult skill to develop and a vital skill for a team leader or supervisor. In this section we will look at how you can become more self-aware, so that you understand how you are perceived by others to help you in your role.

While we may think we are aware of our self and the impact of our actions, we are not always realistic and are not always aware of unconscious bias. This bias, or influence of perceived ideas, is when we are not aware of the effects of our actions or decisions. You should consider this when you reflect on your own actions and how it impacts on how you work in your job role.

Using self-assessment tools

To help you develop self-awareness, you should use various tools to accurately judge how good you are at different aspects of your role.

Reflection activities

The first type of tools you can use are **reflection** activities. Using these, you can look back at what you have done in your role and reflect on what went well, what went badly and areas where you could improve. This will help you to accurately judge your performance and identify ways you can improve.

These activities are not just individual tasks. You could talk through your performance with a line manager. Use this feedback to help you prepare for your competency-based interview and professional discussion in your end point assessment (EPA). You could also keep a reflective diary, logging your daily activities and your thoughts on your performance. This also would provide some useful evidence for your portfolio.

SWOT analysis

A SWOT analysis is an analytical tool that will help you reflect on your own performance. You consider the strengths and weaknesses of your performance as a team leader or supervisor. You then consider the external factors that will influence your performance in the opportunities and threats. Table 1 shows an example of a SWOT analysis to help you undertake your own.

Strengths	Weaknesses
List all the things you are good at, with examples.	List all the things that you are not very good at yet, with examples.
For example:	For example:
I'm good at prioritising tasks. Today I organised the activities my team needed to complete in order of importance.	*I'm not very good at chairing meetings. I had to have a meeting with my team, but I found it hard to keep control and everyone started talking all at once.*
Opportunities	**Threats**
Here, consider the things that may help you that you are not in control of.	Here, consider the things that can go wrong and that you cannot control.
For example:	For example:
I can improve my skills by signing up to extra training at work.	*My organisation is being sold and I am worried about my job.*

Table 1: Undertake a SWOT analysis of your performance

Skills audit

A **skills audit** looks at all the important skills and tasks that are required in your role and asks you to judge how well you can do them; see figure 1. This will help you to identify all the things you can do well and all the things you do less well. You can then start to focus on the things you need to improve.

Personal Skills Audit 1

Student Name: _____   Class: _____

COMMUNICATION SKILLS (Understanding others and making myself understood)	Very Skilled	Moderately Skilled	In Need of Training
1 I am aware of the importance of body language.			
Evidence provided			
2 I can pass on skills to other people.			
Evidence provided			
3 I can find and present information to other people, e.g. to other workers, groups and management.			

Figure 1: Draw up a list of questions for your own skills audit

Learning styles

You will also need to consider your own learning style and those of others. Understanding how you learn will help you become more self-aware and adapt how you work in your role. There are four different types of learning styles for you to consider:

- Visual – People who have a visual learning style like to learn by looking at things. They find looking at pictures or images useful to help them recognise what things mean and remember them.

- Auditory – An auditory learner likes to learn by listening to information, maybe using sound or music. It is important to remember that just using written formats of communication such as those outlined in Section 4 of this handbook may not help an aural learner. You may need to take time to talk through information to help members of your team to understand it.

- Reading/writing – Much of the information in the workplace is provided in writing, such as reports or handbooks. This works well if a learner enjoys reading and writing. However, they may need time to read information and/or write it down to process it.

- Kinaesthetic – Finally, there are people that like to learn by doing. Kinaesthetic learners need to experience something themselves before they fully understand it. You may need to provide opportunities for members of your team to practise aspects of their role.

Analysis of feedback

You can also analyse any feedback that others give you. This will tell you what other people think of you and your skills in your role as team leader or supervisor. Take time to order any feedback into positive and negative views.

Reflecting on outcomes of self-assessment activities

Behaviours

Inclusive – Seeks views of others.

Link to the standard

Knowledge Area 3:
Outcome Topic 1.2

Skills area

Skills Area 3:
Outcome Topic 1

Once you have undertaken self-assessment activities, you can then reflect on their outcomes to help you develop self-awareness about your skills, qualities and behaviours. This involves giving the outcomes careful thought and consideration.

Own skills

After reflecting on the outcome of a skills audit, you can now start to decide what skills you have developed well and what you need to develop further. Start to consider how you can develop these skills; this might involve further training or working with someone who has extensive experience of the skill. Keep notes of what you do to help you in your professional discussion at your end point assessment.

Knowledge and behaviours

You can also judge the level of your knowledge in different aspects of your role. There is a lot to learn when you start a new role and you are likely to have gaps in your knowledge. Once you have identified these, look at how and where you can find out the information you need. Review your behaviours. How do you act or behave in the workplace? You may realise that you need to adapt your behaviour in certain situations to effectively achieve your goals. You should be open and honest with yourself, which sometimes can be difficult to do.

Which quality standards are used in your organisation?

Productivity

Productivity is the measure of the output of individuals, teams or organisations. In reviewing self-assessment tools, evaluate your productivity and that of your team. This analysis will start to tell you how effective you are in your role and highlight where you need to make improvements. You may need to look at different working practices to help you and your team become more efficient. Reviewing how other people in a similar role work may help you gather some ideas.

Quality standards

Each organisation works to a set of quality standards. These are the standards to which products or services are made or delivered to satisfy the needs of customers. These may be externally set, such as ISO 9001 or Investors in People, or internally set standards that the organisation expects you to achieve. During your self-assessment you can judge your performance by looking at how you meet these standards. Failing to meet standards is a serious problem as you will not be meeting the needs of your customers and this may impact on the reputation of the organisation.

Working practices

During the self-assessment process, you can also review your **working practices**. These are the established ways of completing tasks or activities in the workplace. The various policies and procedures within your organisation might determine some of these practices. You may not be able to change these working practices easily, but you may be able to make some suggestions for more effective working.

You will develop your own working practices, and therefore have the freedom to change and adapt these if you feel that they are not working as effectively and efficiently as you would like. Feedback from others may also tell you that you need to work differently. Although the working practice might work well for you, it may be causing issues in other areas of the organisation.

Key term

Working practices – The ways in which tasks and activities are undertaken at work.

Identifying areas of improvement

When reflecting on the outcomes of self-assessment, you may find that you could improve some of the things you do. As a team leader or supervisor, it is important to act as a good role model to others and therefore you need to strive to be the best you can be, at all aspects of your role. It is important to identify areas for improvement. Think of ways to improve these areas and prioritise the most important issues first.

Identifying areas for development

You will also identify skills that you need to develop; skills you do not yet have but need, in order to do your job. You may need to undertake further training to help you develop these skills or find someone else in the organisation who can help you to develop them further.

Recognising achievements and successes

As well as recognising that you have skills that need improving and skills that you need to develop, you should also recognise your strengths. Acknowledge your achievements within your role as a team leader or supervisor. Make sure that you record and recognise these achievements and successes and reference them in your professional discussion at your end point assessment.

Identifying sources of feedback

Aside from gaining feedback from individuals, you will also want to consider who within your organisation can give you useful and realistic feedback. Think about anyone else outside the organisation who you have dealt with that can help provide feedback on your performance.

Table 2 provides some ideas of people you could ask for feedback on your role of team leader or supervisor.

Source of feedback	
Team members	These people work with you closely and are in a good position to give feedback on your performance in your role. Remember that you are in a position of authority within the team and some of your team members may be anxious about being honest with you, possibly worried about any offence their feedback may cause. Others may be overly negative about your performance if you have had issues with their performance or have experienced situations of conflict in the past. Be realistic about how useful this feedback may or may not be.
Line manager	You will have a close working relationship with your line manager and they will have some responsibility for supporting you through your apprenticeship. Therefore, you can ask your line manager to give feedback on your performance and ask them to help you in finding ways to improve upon your performance and develop your skills.
Senior management	You may have undertaken a specific task or project with senior management and therefore they may have first-hand experience of your skills in your role. However, you they may not have had many opportunities to work with them and they may not be able to give you much feedback on your performance. All organisations work differently and you should think about how often you interact with senior management and decide how appropriate asking for their feedback may be.
Other teams and departments	You may be involved in working with other people for other teams and departments and they can offer feedback on your performance. Consider which things they can feedback upon and how you can gather this feedback.

Customers	When working with customers, you have the opportunity to ask them for feedback. Think about what you are going to ask and how you are going to do it. Ensure you do not take too much of the customer's time and that they feel comfortable in giving feedback. Some organisations automatically ask customers to provide feedback after they have provided their service. If this is the case in your organisation, you could use this feedback to help you judge how well you are performing.
Suppliers	You may also work with suppliers, ordering stock, etc. If you do, you could ask them to provide feedback, remembering that they are busy, working in different organisations.
Stakeholders	You may interact with other stakeholders in the organisation. For example, you may be involved in working in the community or with other businesses in the area. Representatives of these groups could offer feedback on the service you have provided and your skills.

Table 2: Ideas for collecting feedback on your performance

When gathering feedback, be aware of unconscious bias and inclusivity. Sometimes we are unconsciously biased. This means that we have perceived ideas and opinions, but are not always aware that these influence the decisions we make. When gathering and using feedback from others, consider whether the views of the people you asked are biased or are objective. Are you unconsciously biased and seeking feedback to support your own opinion?

Consider inclusivity by looking at whether you are gathering feedback from everyone involved and treating each person fairly and equally. It is important to be inclusive in the workplace and not favour one group or individual over another.

What was the last feedback you received? How was it communicated?

Types of feedback sought

Behaviours

Takes responsibility
– Drive to achieve in all
aspects of work.

Key terms

Constructive criticism –
Well-reasoned and valid
feedback, based on both
positives and negatives.
**Appraisal/performance
management review**
– An ongoing process
to review and evaluate
the performance of
employees.

**Link to the
standard**

Knowledge Area 3:
Outcome Topic 1

Skills area

Skills Area 3:
Outcome Topic 1

You need to think about the types of feedback you are seeking as well as where you can obtain it.

Table 3 provides some types of feedback to consider.

Positive feedback	It is always encouraging to be told you are doing a good job. It helps to motivate and reassures you that you are doing the right thing.
Constructive criticism	You will want to know when you are not meeting the standards required or have not developed and demonstrated the skills needed in your role, but you need this feedback to be **constructive**. Feedback should be well balanced, valid and well-reasoned, focusing on positives and negatives and based on evidence. Give those you are gathering feedback from some information on what you are trying to find out, so they focus on the correct aspects of your role.
Performance targets	In your role, you will be set performance targets. This includes the apprenticeship standards outcomes you need to meet to complete your apprenticeship. During your **appraisal/performance management review**, you are likely to be given performance targets. This is the ongoing process of reviewing and evaluating your performance in your role.
Quality standards	Your organisation will have set quality standards that you must achieve. You can use these standards to self-assess your own performance in your role.
Achievement of learning and development goals and objectives	While completing your apprenticeship, there will be a number of learning and development goals and objectives. This includes understanding all the knowledge areas in this handbook, as well as developing and demonstrating the skill and behaviour standard outcomes against which you will be judged in your end point assessment.
Customer complaints	Sometimes things go wrong and customers make complaints. These may be issues, such as waiting times, a faulty product or poor customer service. These complaints reflect on you and your team and you can use them to identify where you can improve things. Remember that as a team leader or supervisor, you are responsible for the performance of your team and yourself.
Customer recognition	Customer recognition refers to the customers' views about the value of the organisation, its products and the service they receive. Unless directly asked to comment on the quality of their experience, customers will not offer it. Unlike when things go wrong, we tend not to hear when things have gone well for customers. Develop methods to collate customer recognition. This could be through surveys and talking to customers about the quality of the service they have received.

Table 3: Which types of feedback have you considered?

Using the feedback received

Once you have gathered feedback, consider how valid it is and how to use it.

- How open and honest have people providing the feedback been?

- Have they understood what they have been asked to feed back on?

- Are they able to provide enough detail in the feedback?

Consider if there is any bias in the feedback provided. It may have come from someone you are friends with and might be overly positive or it may be someone you have experienced conflict with and their feedback might be overly negative.

In doing so, be aware of emotional intelligence when reviewing and using feedback. Be aware of your own emotions and express them appropriately. You may receive feedback that you do not like or feel is unfair. It would be easy in such situations to react by questioning and confronting the person who has offered the feedback. However, as a team leader or supervisor you will need to control your emotions, and take on board everyone's opinions and use them effectively. Emotional intelligence also involves being able to handle interpersonal relationships (relationships with other people) with empathy. You will therefore need to consider how and why the people offering the feedback feel the way they do, trying to put yourself in their position and understand their points of view.

Identify areas where feedback shows changes are needed. Identify the improvements and developments you need to make to your skills and knowledge.

What kind of feedback are you looking for?

>>>>> **Making timely changes**

Think about how quickly you can make changes; see table 4. You might need to prioritise the most important things to do first. Here are some questions which will help you prioritise.

- How important are the skills or knowledge to you and your role?
- What impact will changes have on your organisation?
- How easy is it to acquire a skill or learn the knowledge?

Immediate	• The change is easy to do and you can do it straight away. • Developing or improving the skill or level of knowledge is vital to your role.
Earliest opportunity	• You need to make the change as soon as you can as it will help you significantly in your role. • It may be a change to something that you do not do very often.
When convenient to do so	• These are likely to be minor changes and those that may not have so much of a significant impact on you, your team or the organisation. • This is more likely to be where you are making improvements to skills or knowledge.
When appropriate to do so	• If the change is a large one or one that will impact on other people's roles in the organisation, it may be better to wait to introduce the change to avoid disruption in the workplace.

Table 4: Which changes need to happen first?

Applying learning

It is not sufficient just to learn the information provided in each of the knowledge areas or read about how to develop the different skills areas. You need to apply this learning to your day to day role and use it to fulfil your job role and improve your skills. Start to divide the skills required in your job role into three areas.

1. **Skills you need or work practices you have, but which are ineffective and need developing**
   These should be your priority to develop. These skills are important in your job role and need developing as soon as you can. This is especially important if they are part of the apprenticeship standard criteria, as you must demonstrate that you can do these effectively in order to pass your end point assessment.

2. **Existing skills you have which need enhancing or improving**
   This is the second group of skills you should focus on. They will be things that you can do but need to improve. Practise them as often as you can. Try and observe others using these skills well, to help you improve them.

3. **New skills that you can develop**
   These are other skills that are not vital to your role that would be useful to develop in the future.

How do you apply feedback to develop your self awareness?

Demonstrating appropriate behaviours

You will also need to demonstrate appropriate behaviours at work when developing your self-awareness. We have signposted the behaviours that you should display when undertaking your role as a team leader or supervisor, at different points through this handbook.

Table 5 lists the appropriate behaviours that you need to display when developing self-awareness.

Being resilient	Being resilient involves not giving up and being determined to succeed. Adopt this behaviour when assessing yourself and receiving feedback from others. At times some of the things you are told about yourself might be difficult to hear or developing some of the skills required might be hard to do. Resilience will help you to keep on working toward your end goals, in spite of how hard this might be.
Positively responding to feedback	Take on board all the feedback provided and respond positively to it. You may feel disheartened or upset at times if the feedback is not as good as you would have liked, but you must not take this personally. Don't focus on the negative comments, think positively about the actions you can take to improve.
Positively challenging feedback to clarify understanding	Sometimes, you may not fully understand the feedback given or you need further information to. You need to positively challenge the feedback given and ask questions to clarify what is meant by the comments made. This does not mean that you should argue about the feedback given but ask for examples of when and where you have lacked the skills required.

Table 5: Do you behave like this?

Summary

In this section you have learned how to be self-aware and to understand unconscious bias. This section has covered:
- the self-assessment tools, and sources and types of feedback, that can help you in developing your own skills
- how to make changes by applying learning from feedback received.

Activities

▶ **Activity 1**

Think about all the skills and qualities that are important in your role. Produce a skills audit and complete it, judging your own performance. You can also ask others within the organisation to complete the skills audit for you and compare your responses with theirs. This will help you judge how well you do things but also how self-aware you are about your performance in your role.

▶ **Activity 2**

Think about all the people you work with, in your role at work. These could be people within the organisation, such as your line manager or members of your team or people outside the business such as customers or other stakeholders.

Make a list of whom you could ask for feedback on your role and skills. Think about how you could gather feedback from them and which aspects of your role they could make comments on.

▶ **Activity 3**

Consider the types of feedback that you can gather. Look at the different types of feedback that are available to you and start to make a list of all the types of feedback you can gather. Once you have done this, think about how you will use the feedback provided.

▶ **Activity 4**

Consider the skills you need to use on a day to day basis in your job. Also, make a list of the different skills that are involved in the apprenticeship standard outcomes that you will be assessed against in your end point assessment.

Think about the skills that you need to develop or improve under the following headings:

1. The skills or practices that you need but are currently sub-standard and need developing

2. Existing skills that you have but need to enhance or improve

3. Ideas for new skills that you could use that have been suggested in the apprenticeship standard outcomes or in this handbook

Once you have created the three lists of skills, start to think about how you can develop them.

Topic consolidation

▶ Test yourself

1. Consider how well you perform in your job role. How would you rate your performance?

   ☐ excellent
   ☐ good
   ☐ requires improvement
   ☐ inadequate

2. Think about a time when you have had to make changes based on feedback provided by others. Did you act:

   ☐ immediately
   ☐ at the earliest opportunity
   ☐ when convenient to do so
   ☐ when appropriate to do so?

3. When receiving feedback from others, do you:

   ☐ listen and take on board the feedback
   ☐ act on every piece of feedback offered
   ☐ listen to the feedback but ignore it
   ☐ be offended by the comments made by others?

4. In your organisation, who would be best to ask for feedback:

   ☐ your team
   ☐ your line manager
   ☐ your customers
   ☐ other team leaders or supervisors?

5. At times you need resilience when assessing yourself and receiving feedback. How do you adopt this behaviour?

   ☐ extremely well
   ☐ very well
   ☐ requires improvement
   ☐ inadequately

6. How would you rate your ability to identify areas for self-development?

   ☐ excellent
   ☐ good
   ☐ requires improvement
   ☐ inadequate

9

Management of self

What is management of self?

Managing one's self is an important skill in the workplace. We have already discussed your management of others in the workplace and how to develop your team; this section is about how to manage yourself.

Self-management refers to how you organise yourself and prioritise tasks. It involves taking responsibility for your own actions and the things you do. It is also about personal development. This means developing yourself to be the best you can. There are a number of self-management techniques and tools that you can use to help manage yourself and we will discuss these in this section.

Producing a personal development plan

Key terms

Personal development plan (PDP) – A plan outlining the objectives, activities and support of personal development.

Goals – Long-term targets you want to achieve.

Objectives – Measurable steps you must take to achieve a strategy or goal.

Behaviours

Professionalism – Open and honest.

Link to the standard

Skills Area 3: Outcome Topic 2

The first useful tool you can use to help manage yourself, the workload and pressure of your job is a **personal development plan (PDP)**; see figure 1. This document plans out what you what to achieve, the steps you must take to achieve it and the activities/support required to help you do this. It also includes a timescale for the achievement of your **goals** and **objectives** to help you to prioritise the activities involved and manage your time.

Personal Development Plan

Name: _____   Start date: _____

End date: _____

Goal What do I want to achieve?	Actions What do I need to do to achieve them?	Key milestones When and how will I monitor my progress?	Outcomes How will I know they have been achieved?

Figure 1: Start to build your own personal development plan

There are a number of different sections of the plan you should consider.

Identifying learning and development goals and objectives

The first thing you need to do is to identify learning development goals and objectives. These are the targets you set yourself for your future learning and development. They can be things that you want to learn or skills/strategies you want to develop. There may also be a specific career goal, such as becoming a section manager in five years.

The objectives are the measurable steps that you should take to achieve your goal. These could be things you need to learn, such as organisational policies and procedures or specific skills, such as improving verbal communication skills.

Identifying action points

Once you have identified the learning and development goals and objectives, identify the action points required to help you achieve them. Break these down into clear steps and think about how you will achieve each step.

Identifying learning and development activities

Consider what learning and development activities you can use to help you in completing the actions. These activities could cover a range of different things, including shadowing another team leader or supervisor, attending in-house or external training events, or learning more about different aspects of the knowledge areas in this handbook. You may want to brainstorm ideas and share the ideas with your line manager or other people to gather feedback.

Identifying persons responsible

Who can provide support and help you achieve your objectives and goals? Are they willing and able to help you? Identify people who can help you and confirm that they are able to help.

Identifying resources required

Make a list of resources that you need to help you with the actions or activities and where and when you can access them.

Agreeing timescales for achievement

Finally, agree a timescale for the achievement of the goals and objectives, and ensure that this is realistic and manageable. You can then start prioritising the completion of the activities or actions to help you ensure that you make the progress you need.

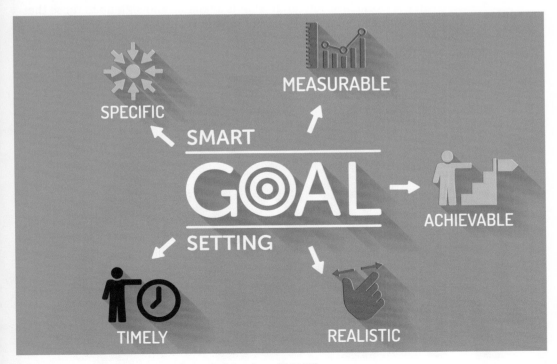

Remember to make your goals and objectives SMART.

Learning and development objectives

Behaviours

Inclusive – Open, approachable, authentic and able to build trust with others.

Link to the standard

Skills Area 3: Outcome Topic 2

Depending on which skills, knowledge or behaviours you need to develop, you may agree different learning and development objectives. These must be specific to you and your own learning and development needs.

Table 1 details some learning and development objectives for you to consider. These are only examples and you need to establish your own that are appropriate to you.

Achievement of industry qualifications	There are a number of different industry qualifications relating to your role as a team leader or supervisor. For example, you might want to study for a Professional Certificate in Team Leadership or a Diploma in Team Leadership and Management. A number of companies and providers offer similar qualifications. You may also consider different industry specific qualifications that you could study for, which are related to the industry you work in.
Attendance of training courses	Training courses help develop your skills and knowledge. These will have a specific focus and help you develop in a certain aspect of your role.
Completing online in-house learning modules	Your organisation may offer in-house learning modules. These are short courses, sometimes online, that the organisation offers to its employees to be completed at their own pace. They could cover things such as customer service skills, valuing diversity or health and safety in the workplace. Research what is available and sign up to those that are interesting or will be useful in your role.

Table 1: Example objectives

What opportunities to attend training courses do you have?

Learning and development goals

Table 2 details different skills you may want to develop and include in your learning and development goals.

Soft skills	Soft skills are those that help you work professionally and work well with others. They include aspects of your personality and emotional intelligence but also skills that you can further develop. Examples include communication skills, empathy, team-working and decision-making. They are also more practical skills, such as good timekeeping or learning how to drive. Soft skills are additional skills that will help you develop, improve your performance in your role and make you stand out from others, when you are considering career progression.
Work-specific skills and knowledge	There will be other work-specific skills and knowledge that are only relevant to your role. You may already have some of these skills and knowledge, but may need to develop others. Consider the work-related skills and knowledge you have and which skills need further development. These can include the development of more complex work-specific skills that are more challenging or need more practice. They can also involve learning new processes, ways of doing things, preparing for or applying for a promotion.

Table 2: Which skills do you need to develop?

Key terms

Soft skills – Transferable or professional skills.

Work-specific skills – The skills related to your specific job role.

How do you use soft skills in your role?

Monitoring a personal development plan

Behaviours **B**

Agile – Positive and adaptable, responds well to feedback and need to change.

Link to the standard

Skills Area 3: Outcome Topic 2

Once you have developed your personal development plan (PDP), it is vital to monitor your progress toward your objectives and goals. You need to regularly check your progress in achieving your objectives and goals, focusing on the following areas to help you.

Set review dates

Set review dates at regular intervals to allow you time to review how well you are doing. Look at the different activities you should have undertaken and check whether they have been done. If they haven't consider whether you still need to do them and if so, set a new date for them to be achieved.

Recording achievement

Record any achievements toward your goals and targets you have made in the time provided. Keep a note of these as you achieve them so you don't forget to include them when you review your plan. Remember that the plan and your achievements will be useful when completing your end point assessment (EPA). Records of achievement provide evidence of the criterion achieved and give you some ideas of what to discuss during your professional discussion.

Recording feedback from appraisals and personal reviews

During the year, you will be given feedback during appraisals and personal reviews. This feedback could be linked to your PDP, allowing you to check this against your progress and sign off some of your goals and objectives. Using your PDP in these reviews will help you demonstrate how you are developing and what you plan to do to develop further.

Use your PDP as a focus for your appraisals and reviews

Reviewing and revising objectives

As you progress, some of your objectives may need revising or adapting. You may have been overly ambitious when you originally set them, or you may have already achieved an objective and need to change it to something else or to something more challenging.

Tracking against targets (milestones, completion)

When setting your objectives and goals, set targets for completion and key **milestones**. Milestones are things you want to achieve along the way by certain dates. When you review your PDP, look at these milestones and completion dates and judge whether you have achieved them or not. If you haven't achieved them by the dates originally set, adjust them and agree new targets for their completion. Be aware of the dates set and review them regularly to help you keep your plan on track for a timely and successful completion.

Key term

Milestones – Significant stages in developing a plan or project.

Identifying reasons for deviations from plan

As you work towards the goals and objectives in your plan, things may not go as you expected. While you should stick to your plan as much as possible, you also need to be realistic and adapt your plan when needed. Sometimes things out of your control change and you will be unable to complete the activities set or achieve the original timescale. Keep a note or record of deviations and be prepared to provide reasons for them to explain why things have changed and your plans have altered.

Identifying exploitable or corrective actions

When things change or go wrong, it is important you do not give up or assume an opportunity has passed. Look at what has changed or gone wrong and implement corrective actions to try and make successful completion possible. As things change and develop in your job role and organisation, new opportunities may become available for you to exploit and you may want to include these in your PDP.

Overall it is important to remember that your PDP is just a plan and all plans change. It is totally acceptable to change things but make sure you keep it up to date as you go along. See your plan as a working document, something that should be reviewed, updated and changed as you work through the process. Agree changes with your line manager.

Managing workload

Working as a team leader or supervisor is a busy role with lots of tasks to complete daily. Sometimes this may feel overwhelming and you may not be able to get everything done. At other times, you may not feel you have much to do and feel unmotivated. It is important you manage your workload, planning out what you will do and when.

Some tips on how to manage your workload effectively are shown in figure 2 and table 3. Being proactive and getting things done before deadlines will help you even out your workload. Remember, as a team leader or supervisor, you will be responsible for managing your team's workload. Be aware of and plan their individual workloads to help you ensure that all the tasks and activities you are responsible for get done on time.

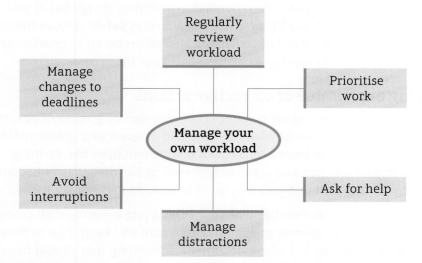

Figure 2: Some ideas about how you can manage your own workload

Management	Actions
Regularly review workload	• Review your own and your team's workloads. • Plan what needs doing and by when. • Identify busy periods. • Find solutions if deadlines are missed.
Prioritise work	• Identify the most important or urgent tasks. • Review the impact of the task on the organisation. • Communicate timescales to your team.
Ask for help	• Remember that everyone feels overwhelmed at times and that you are part of a team. • Members of your team or other colleagues have the skills, knowledge and, most importantly, time to help you. • Don't be afraid to ask! • They may need your help in future and good teamwork is needed to ensure that everything is completed on time.
Manage distractions	• Keep personal communications for breaks. • Focus on the tasks you need to do that day. • As a team leader or supervisor, you should be a positive role model and if your team see you being professional, they are more likely to act in a similar manner. • Complete the task in hand before moving on to something else (unless urgent).
Avoid interruptions	• Let others know that you are working on something and don't want to be disturbed. • Remove yourself, if you can, from any potential interruptions, such as finding a quiet office space to focus on the task.
Manage changes to deadlines	• Deadlines can change, and it is important that you keep track of these changes to make sure that you are working to the correct timescale. • If the deadline is extended, you may need to review your priorities to see if something else needs doing first. • If the deadline is brought forward, look at all your other work and find the time to work on this task first to make sure it gets done in time.

Table 3: Try these ideas to help you manage your workload

Prioritising tasks according to situation

Put the tasks and activities you need to complete in order of urgency; how quickly does it need to be done and who will it affect if it is not completed on time? Consider the importance of the task or activity. Is it vital to the organisation? Is it a minor task that does not really affect how the business works? Finally, think about the consequences of completing the task or activity late. Will it stop others completing their tasks effectively? Will it delay products or services reaching customers? Will it mean that the organisation cannot function effectively and meet its objectives?

Appropriate behaviours

Developing different behaviours will help you in your role and in meeting the apprenticeship standards.

Be resilient to change

Changes might make you feel frustrated or confused. Developing resilience to change will help you to remain focused and respond to changes calmly. Your team will look to you to see how to manage change and therefore you must demonstrate confidence to achieve tasks.

Problem solve

Learn how to find solutions to the problems that might arise each day at work, thinking them through to ensure that they will work effectively.

Meet commitments

Being reliable and dependable is important as a team leader or supervisor, as your team rely on you and your line manager needs to know that you will make sure that the job will get done. Ensure that you do what you say you will do and say when you will do it.

Be organised

Show that you are in control of the tasks and activities allocated to you and your team and demonstrate that you can organise yourself to make sure that tasks are completed.

Maintain focus

Demonstrate that you can maintain focus on the task at hand and not get distracted. This will take effort and concentration, using some of the strategies and techniques outlined in table 3 on page 179.

Remain positive

As a team leader or supervisor, you will be responsible for motivating your team and presenting a positive image of your organisation. Being pleasant and positive in the workplace is important to your effectiveness in your role.

Using time management tools

Managing your time can be difficult, especially if you have a lot of things to do. It is easy to forget things or spend too much time on one task. You will develop a preferred way of managing your time but here are some suggested management tools that you could use. You may want to try them out to see which works best for you.

Calendars

Using a calendar to mark on or highlight tasks can be an effective way of managing your time. You can use a printed calendar displayed in the area where you work so you, and others, see what you are doing and when, or use an electronic or online calendar. Many email systems have these. Alternatively you may have access to a central calendar, used in your organisation. Again, you can share your calendar with others and access it from smartphones or other devices.

Schedules

You can also use a schedule to help you plan out your time. A schedule is a timetable, that plans out what you are doing and when each day, week or month. You will have been used to using a schedule or timetable at school, so you might find this helps you.

Diary

A diary is a book or electronic tool that plans out and records events and activities each day. This can be useful as it stores all the information in one place and helps you track your progress. You can also use it to record how long activities and tasks have taken you and what tasks are required on certain days, weeks or months during the year. This provides a valuable record. Therefore, once you have completed and used a diary in the first year, you can use it to help you plan for the following year.

'To do' list

A 'to-do' list can be very useful in helping you manage your workload. This is a simple list of the tasks or activities you need to complete during the day or week, sometimes put in order of priority. You can easily see how many things you have to do and in what order, letting you tick them off as you complete them. Seeing what you have done can be motivating. There are many web-based or app-based tools to use too, which can be helpful when working in teams or on larger projects

Behaviours

Takes responsibility – Demonstrates resilience and accountability.

Link to the standard

Knowledge Area 3: Outcome Topic 2

Skills Area 3: Outcome Topic 2

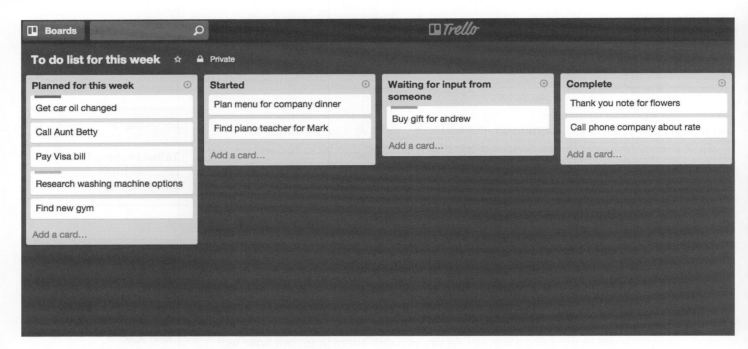

How could online tools like this help you in your role?

Summary

In this section you have learned how to produce, use and manage personal development plans to help you develop your skills and behaviours at work. This section has covered:

- managing your own workload
- prioritising your time
- using time management techniques and tools to manage your workload and pressure at work

Activities

▶ Activity 1

Produce your own PDP. You may want to reflect on the skills audit you produced when developing your own self-assessment. Ask your line manager to contribute to, or comment on, your plan, so you are sure you are identifying the right goals and objectives and you include all the correct activities and support.

▶ Activity 2

Research your organisation for the different opportunities for:

- achievement of industry qualifications
- attendance of training courses
- completing online in-house learning modules.

Which are available to you? How long will they take? What do they involve and at what cost? Would your organisation support you undertaking them?

▶ Activity 3

Think about the skills you need to develop in your role and those you may include as goals in your PDP.

What soft skills and work-related skills do you need to develop?

▶ Activity 4

Consider a usual working week or month in your job role.

- What tasks or activities do you need to complete?
- Are some days/times busier for you than others?
- How do you go about managing your workload?
- What time management techniques could help you in future?

Use one of the time management techniques in this section to help you plan your workload during this week or month.

▶ Activity 5

Reflecting on the week or month you have focused on in Activity 4. Choose one or two of the following time management tools and try them to help you plan out your time during this period:

- calendars
- schedules
- diary
- 'to do' list.

Topic consolidation

▶ Test yourself

1. How did you feel at work today:

   ☐ overwhelmed
   ☐ stressed
   ☐ in control
   ☐ bored?

2. How would you rate your ability to manage your own time?

   ☐ excellent
   ☐ good
   ☐ requires improvement
   ☐ inadequate

3. When managing the workload of your team, do you:

   ☐ prioritise your own tasks and responsibilities
   ☐ take too much on yourself to help out others
   ☐ leave everyone else to their own work
   ☐ review workloads regularly and make changes when needed?

4. While at work this week have you:

   ☐ managed your own workload effectively
   ☐ run out of time but got everything done
   ☐ not managed to complete everything you needed to do
   ☐ had to ask others for help to complete the tasks required?

5. To help you manage your own time at work, do you prefer to use:

   ☐ a calendar
   ☐ a schedule
   ☐ a diary
   ☐ a 'to do' list?

6. How would you rate your ability to ask for help when needed?

   ☐ excellent
   ☐ good
   ☐ requires improvement
   ☐ inadequate

10

Decision-making

What is decision-making?

Decision-making is an important skill for a team leader or supervisor to develop. You will need to make decisions about how you and your team carry out the tasks you are allocated. You will have to make decisions about who will do what and when they should do it.

Improving your decision-making skills and developing appropriate problem-solving techniques to help you make well informed decisions is key to your role. You will also need to learn how to use information from others to inform decision-making and the steps used to make effective decisions.

>>>>> **Problem-solving techniques**

Behaviours **B**

Takes responsibility – Determination when managing difficult situations.

Link to the standard

Knowledge Area 3: Outcome Topic 3

Skills Area 3: Outcome Topic 3

Key terms

Brainstorming – Developing and analysing creative ideas.

Workshops – Meetings to hold intensive discussion and analysis of a project or idea.

In your role as team leader or supervisor you will be faced with different problems that need to be solved effectively and efficiently. Here are a number of different techniques you can use to help you solve problems.

Brainstorming

Brainstorming involves developing ideas either on your own or working with your team. Everyone involved is encouraged to contribute as many ideas as they can regardless of how extreme or ambitious they seem. The ideas are then discussed by everyone, analysing the pros and cons of each one and evaluating which ideas are the best.

Workshops

A **workshop** is a meeting with one item on the agenda. It focuses on an intensive discussion about a project or idea. Workshops can be useful when you need to make decisions about what you and your team are going to do. You can get everyone involved together in one room and discuss all the aspects of the project or idea, agreeing exactly what is going to be done and by who. You can also discuss and solve any problems you come across there and then, so it may make the process faster and more effective.

SWOT analysis

A SWOT analysis allows you to consider the strengths and weaknesses of a project or idea, alongside the opportunities and threats that may affect it from external factors. You can therefore start to decide whether the project or idea is worthwhile and what you should to do to avoid the identified weaknesses and threats to make it successful.

Use a SWOT analysis on one of your projects

PESTLE analysis

PESTLE analysis is a decision-making tool that helps you analyse the effect of factors outside the organisation on the project or idea. It focuses on six groups of factors.

Table 1 is an example of PESTLE analysis which will help you understand further what each of the different factors entails.

Political	Economic
These are policies or initiatives the government introduces or actions they take that affect your project or idea. For example, taxation, business policies, etc.	These are factors related to the economy of the country. For example, rate of **inflation**, standards of living, consumer spending and **economic growth**.
Social	Technological
These are factors related to society or the population of the country. For example, trends and fashions, **demographics** and changes in lifestyle.	These are factors that involve changes or improvements in technology. For example, new production processes, new products, innovation in markets, improvements in mobile technology.
Legal	Ethical/environmental
These factors relate to laws and legislations put in place by the government. For example, health and safety laws, the minimum wage and employment law.	These are factors that affect the environment. For example, pollution or impact on the carbon footprint. It also includes ethical issues. For example, buying from suppliers that treat their workers fairly.

Table 1: Factors considered in a PESTLE analysis

Risk analysis

Risk analysis is a tool to identify all the things that can go wrong with a project or idea. Ask two questions: firstly, how likely is it that this will happen? Secondly, what can you do to avoid it? Based on your answers you can decide whether it is worth undertaking the project or idea and what you need to do to avoid the risks and make sure it is successful.

Root cause analysis (RCA)

RCA is a tool that can be used to identify the cause of a problem, so that you can find ways to solve it. To complete an RCA, identify the main areas that cause the problem to arise and then work through every aspect of the area to find out where the problem is arising and why.

Pareto principle

The Pareto principle is also known as the 80/20 rule. It says that 80 per cent of the effects come from 20 per cent of causes. It demonstrates that often when things go wrong, the causes are relatively small and could be relatively easy to solve. When things go wrong, you can feel overwhelmed and start to panic but the Pareto principle helps you put this into perspective.

Behaviours

Agile – Is creative, innovative and enterprising when seeking solutions to business needs

Link to the standard

Knowledge Area 3: Outcome Topic 3

Skills Area 3: Outcome Topic 3

PDCA

This is an approach you can take to planning out what you are going to do and how to do it. PDCA stands for **P**lan, **D**o, **C**heck, **A**ct as in figure 1.

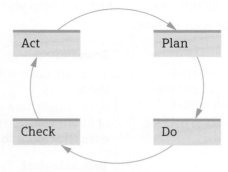

Figure 1: The PDCA approach

1. **Plan**: Start by planning out what you need to do, what you want to achieve and gather the information you need to make your decision

2. **Do**: Once you have planned it out, develop an appropriate strategy and test it.

3. **Check**: Check whether the strategy has been successful and review its outcome.

4. **Act**: Finally, if the strategy in the test worked, implement it. If not, repeat the process until you find an effective strategy.

5 Whys analysis

This is a strategy that involves you asking yourself five questions all starting with why? As you answer each question, the answer then creates a new question. This will finally lead you to the root of the problem so that you can solve it. See figure 2 for an example of these questions.

Figure 2: Use this approach with a current problem you face at work

Using problem-solving techniques

Sometimes you may need to create new ideas of ways of working, ideas for projects or even for new products or services. You will have already made a lot of decisions in your role as team leader or supervisor but you may feel that you were not as effective as you could be in the process. Practise and use some of the following techniques to help you improve on the quality of the decisions you make and the decision-making process.

Behaviours B

Inclusive – Seeks views of others.

Link to the standard

Knowledge Area 3: Outcome Topic 3

Skills Area 3: Outcome Topic 3

Analysis customer feedback

Customers can be a vital source of information for informing your decisions. Customers are an important stakeholder for your organisation and you need to take their views seriously. Positive feedback is useful to reinforce your current practices but negative feedback regarding products, quality of service, or about a member of your team is also key. Reflect on this feedback and use it to make decisions about what needs changing and what you need to do.

Monitoring data

As a team leader or supervisor, you will have access to your organisation's data about its staff. You can use this to inform decisions about how to use your team effectively and actions you need to make to deal with issues. Here are some examples of information about your team.

- Quality checks with staff: Collect and use information about the quality of your team's work. Sample items they have produced or check in with them on a shift to see how things are going. Most organisations formalise this and provide records of outcomes to provide evidence towards performance reviews, etc.

- Observations of staff to reveal potential trends in service failure: This will help you identify issues and then you can use this information to help staff correct the issues. You may also need to decide if you should escalate the issue to someone more senior.

Benchmarking

Many organisations **benchmark** against their competitors. They look at the performance, actions and strategies of other organisations in their industry and compare their own organisation to them. This helps set standards and objectives that are appropriate to their industry and identify good ideas to implement. The organisation may also have its own standards or wider industry standards they can benchmark their performance against. All of this information is useful to help you make decisions about your team and find new, improved ways of doing things.

Key term

Benchmarking – Measuring the organisation's performance against the best organisations in the industry.

Service level agreements (SLAs) and identifying service failures

SLAs are contracts between the service provider (the person who provides the service or product) and the end user (the customer or other department of the organisation who uses the service or product). It agrees the level of service expected, including the standard of work, timescales and deadlines and any special agreements. You will be aware of any SLAs in place in your organisation and their expectations, and can use them to help you make decisions about what you need to do and when.

Auditing of the supply chain

The supply chain is the process or steps that products go through from the first stage of production to it being received by the end user. You should **audit** this process, checking and analysing all the different stages to evaluate its effectiveness. Look at the quality of service provided by suppliers and whether it meets expectations. If there are any failures in the service provided you need to decide how to respond and act. In addition, consider any service partners your organisation has, such as accounting, marketing and maintenance services. You will also need to audit the services they provide to identify any issues and help you make decisions about your future work with them.

Using information from the team and others to inform decision-making

You will also have the opportunity to gather feedback from your team and wider organisation to help inform your decision-making. This is useful first-hand information from people you know, but be aware that it may not always be the most accurate.

Obtaining sufficient information from reliable sources

If you base decisions on information, you need to make sure that your sources are not biased and can be trusted to give an open and honest view. Ensure that you ask a range of different people in different roles, as their opinions and points of view may differ.

Validating the information received

Once you have gathered all the information you need, ensure that you validate it so you know it is reliable. Check the information to make sure that it is accurate. Table 2 shows you ways to validate the information.

Triangulation	Use two or more sources to check that information is correct.
Credibility of source	Is your source and information trustworthy and reliable?
Accuracy	Check that the information is correct and considers all the different aspects of the topic or situation.
Reasonableness	Sometimes when people or organisations have a strong view on something, their view and opinions can become biased.
Relevance	Check the information is relevant. You may find a lot of facts and information from secondary sources, but little of it may apply to the situation you are experiencing.

Table 2: Use these criteria to validate information

Decision-making steps

When making decisions in your role as a team leader or supervisor, it is important to take a systematic approach. Taking the process step by step and considering every aspect at each stage will help you make a well-reasoned decision as in figure 3.

Behaviours

Professionalism – Operates within organisational values.

Identify the problem → Consider options and solutions → Implement the decision → Monitor and seek feedback on the outcomes

Figure 3: Break down the decision into key parts to help you

Link to the standard

Knowledge Area 3: Outcome Topic 3

Skills Area 3: Outcome Topic 3

Identifying the problem

When identifying a problem there are a number of things to consider.

1. Problem analysis

Undertake problem analysis across all aspects of the problem to identify the causes and effects. This will help you start to think about a solution.

2. Outcomes to be achieved

Identify the outcomes that need to be achieved so you know exactly what you want to accomplish.

3. SMART objectives

Once you have identified the outcomes, you can go further and identify SMART objectives. Making these detailed objectives will help you judge your success at the end of the process.

4. Information gathering

Identify where you can find the information. You can use a range of sources of information, checking their validity.

5. Using management reports and performance indicators

You can use all of this information, where relevant, to help you gather the information you need and gain a good understanding of the issues, problems or situation.

Considering options and solutions

Once you have identified all aspects of the problem, then you can move onto the second stage of the process, where you consider all the options and solutions.

1. Identifying advantages and disadvantages of each option

It is important you do this so you compare them with each other and help you decide which the best one is.

2. Identifying potential problems and risks

Consider how likely they are to occur and how serious the impact they would have on the organisation. This will help you plan to avoid them but also choose the best solution.

3. Performing analysis

Analytical tools to help you examine the options and solutions can be used at this stage.

4. Adopting the recommendation

Once you have considered all of the options, make a recommendation to the organisation or others in the team, outlining the solution or option you think is best and why. You may need to convince others that your recommendation is the right thing to do, so prepare arguments in advance.

5. Making the decision

Once you have adopted the recommendation, make the final decision based on all the information and discussions that have taken place.

6. Taking responsibility for the decision

When you have made the decision, you need to take responsibility for it and do all you can to ensure that it is successful. As a team leader or supervisor, you should stand by the decisions you have made and not blame others if things go wrong.

Implementing the decision

You then need to implement the decision in the third stage of the process.

1. Act on the chosen solution

Put actions in place to carry out the decision. You should organise who will do what and when, checking progress to ensure that the solution is successful.

2. Setting standard operating procedures

Set and agree standard procedures for everyone to use when working to implement the decision. Share these with everyone so your team are aware of how they should be working and to what standard.

3. Setting SMART objectives

Ensure everyone on the team is aware of the overall objectives so they understand what they are working towards. Set each team member their own individual SMART objectives, so they know what they need to do and by when.

4. Identifying additional problems

As you implement the decision, further problems may arise that mean you need to make changes. It is important to identify these problems, ensuring that your team share any issues they face with you, so can put strategies in place to correct them.

Monitoring and seeking feedback on the outcomes

The final stage of decision-making involves monitoring the performance of the solution and seeking feedback on the outcomes.

1. Checking success and achievement against objectives

Check how successful your solution has been, comparing it against the objectives you set to help you judge its achievements. This demonstrates how well you have solved the problem and identifies areas for future improvement.

2. Gaining feedback from users and other stakeholders involved in the process

Feedback from a range of different stakeholders in the process will help you to judge the level of success.

3. Recording outcomes

This might be in a report or document produced for your line manager, or a financial document. You may also want to record the outcomes of the solution to provide evidence for your end point assessment or annual appraisal/performance review.

How do you currently receive feedback from stakeholders?

>>>> **Escalating problems**

Behaviours

Takes responsibility – Drive to achieve in all aspects of work.

Link to the standard

Knowledge Area 3: Outcome Topic 3
Skills Area 3: Outcome Topic 3

Sometimes you will encounter issues that are very serious or you are unsure how to deal with them. You should escalate these problems to someone senior. It is better to escalate the problem or at least discuss with someone else than try and deal with it yourself. You need to talk to your line manager about when and how to escalate problems in the organisation.

Follow escalation procedures

Every organisation will have escalation procedures in place. These are the processes and methods you use to escalate problems and issues. They will outline what situations/issues should be escalated and to who.

Communicating with more senior colleagues

Consider how you communicate with senior colleagues. You may work with some of these colleagues closely and therefore it might be appropriate to approach them informally to discuss the problem. However, you might have little involvement with them and you may need to follow formal and official procedures to escalate the issue.

Explaining the problem

You need to be calm and clear, explaining exactly what has happened and what the problem is. Take time to collect your thoughts and write down a few notes so that you are clear about what you need to say.

Seeking guidance or decisions

Sometimes, rather than just escalating the problem, you could ask for advice or guidance about what you might do to solve the problem. This will help you maintain your authority and ensure that your team maintain their faith in you to make sensible decisions.

Acknowledging levels of authority in the organisation

There will be an organisation structure in place, which outlines who is responsible for what and who has what authority. Be aware of the structure at your organisation, so that you work within these levels of authority.

Do you know the levels of authority in your organisation?

Acknowledging limits of own authority

You will need to agree what you can and cannot do with your line manager and ensure that you work within the limits of your authority.

Limits of knowledge

While you will have some experience in your industry and have developed some knowledge of how it works, there will be gaps in your knowledge and skills. If you don't know something or are unsure, escalate the issue to your line manager or ask for clarification, so you know you are doing the right thing.

When would you talk to your line manager about escalating problems within your organisation?

Handing over control of the situation

Something outside your control may have changed, which means that you cannot handle the situation yourself. In these situations, you may need to hand over control to someone else, who has more experience and authority to sort out the situation and achieve the objectives.

Level and speed of progress

Finally you need to consider what an appropriate level of progress is and how quickly this should be made. As you monitor your progress, you may find that things are moving too slowly. This may mean that you choose to escalate things to someone else to ensure that things move on more quickly.

Summary

In this section you have learned about problem-solving techniques that can be used in the workplace. This section has covered:

- types information that can be used to make decisions and how to use it effectively
- steps in the decision-making process and when and how to escalate problems to others.

Activities

▶ **Activity 1**

Think of a situation at work where you have had to:

* create new ideas
* decide how to carry out a task
* solve a problem.

How did you make the decision as to what to do? What technique or process did you use? What techniques included in this section could you use to help yourself?

▶ **Activity 2**

Next time you have to make a decision, use one of the following techniques to help you make it:

* brainstorming
* PDCA
* SWOT analysis
* PESTLE analysis.

▶ **Activity 3**

Thinking of a time you had to solve a problem at work, use one of the following to practise problem-solving:

* risk analysis
* root cause analysis
* Pareto principle
* 5 whys analysis.

▶ **Activity 4**

What types of information and feedback could you use in and outside your organisation to help you make decisions? How will you make sure that this information is validated and accurate?

▶ **Activity 5**

Think about a decision you need to make at work. Practise using the decision-making steps discussed in this section to help make the decision.

Make a note of the following to help you prepare for your professional discussion and competency-based interview:

* What did you do?
* What went well? What went badly?
* What decision did you make? Was it the correct one?
* What would you do differently next time?

▶ **Activity 6**

Investigate the structure and lines of authority in your organisation. Who would you escalate problems to? What procedure would you use to do this?

Topic consolidation

▶ Test yourself

1. When making decisions at work, do you:

- ☐ find it difficult to decide
- ☐ decide immediately
- ☐ ask others for their opinions first
- ☐ leave it up to someone else to decide?

2. How would you rate your ability to make decisions?

- ☐ excellent
- ☐ good
- ☐ requires improvement
- ☐ inadequate

3. When using information you have gathered, do you:

- ☐ accept the information is correct regardless
- ☐ triangulate the data with other sources
- ☐ ask others whether they think it looks right
- ☐ use information from lots of different stakeholders?

4. When handling problems at work, do you:

- ☐ consult others about what they think you should do
- ☐ use problem-solving techniques to help you think through the problem
- ☐ consider all aspects of the problem, including its causes and effects
- ☐ think of a solution and action it as soon as you can?

5. If you need to escalate a problem to someone more senior, are you:

- ☐ happy and relieved
- ☐ upset and disappointed
- ☐ uncomfortable and awkward
- ☐ disappointed but know it is the right thing to do?

6. How would you rate your ability to escalate a problem when needed?

- ☐ excellent
- ☐ good
- ☐ requires improvement
- ☐ inadequate

11

Continuous professional development (CPD)

How do you continually update your professional development?

A good starting point in developing your skills, knowledge and behaviours at work is to identify and create objectives that you can work towards. These should meet both the organisation's and your own objectives. This will allow you to measure your progression and recognise your achievements. It will also allow you to contribute to the success of your organisation. You will use a wide range of activities for your professional development, based on discussions with your line manager and decisions that you have jointly made and recorded in your personal development plan (PDP). Reflecting on your progress and achievements will enable you to continue your learning and development throughout your career.

SMART objectives

Link to the standard

CPD Professional Discussion band 1.1 and band 2.2

You need to complete a **training needs analysis** (TNA) of your existing skills, knowledge and behaviours and compare your findings to those required to do your job. This will help you to establish your learning and development needs. From these you can create your own objectives. Your objectives should be SMART (see table 1) and linked to those of your organisation and recorded on a document for future reference, such as a PDP.

Key terms

Training needs analysis – A process to identify the gap between the existing skills, knowledge and behaviours of an individual and the skills, knowledge and behaviours required to do their job.

Aspirations – Things that you hope to achieve.

Specific	When setting yourself an objective ensure that it clearly states your aim.
Measurable	Think about how you will measure the success of your objective and how you will recognise when you have achieved it. A measure could be a % improvement, or something less tangible such as completing a programme of learning.
Achievable	When establishing the detail of your objective, ensure that it is attainable and you will be able to meet any deadlines. For example, if your objective is linked to a programme of learning, ensure that you have sufficient time in which to complete it.
Realistic	Do not set yourself up to fail by deciding on objectives that are unrealistic. For example, if you set a measure to increase sales by 80 per cent, ensure that it is possible to achieve this.
Time-bound	Always set a deadline by when you will achieve your objective. This will ensure that you remain focused and motivated to achieve your objectives.

Table 1: SMART objectives

Behaviours

Takes responsibility – Drive to achieve in all aspects of work. Demonstrates resilience and accountability.

Agile – Flexible to the needs of the organisation.

There should be a direct and positive relationship between your SMART learning and development goals and the requirements of your job, your organisational goals and your own career **aspirations**, as shown in figure 1.

Recording your CPD

There are several ways that you can record your CPD, either paper-based, electronic or a combination of both.

Electronic CPD

Recording all your CPD activity into an electronic document will ensure your CPD is organised. You can use a spreadsheet with headings to suit your needs. This would allow you to record the activities you have undertaken and your reflection of each.

You can create an electronic folder of course handouts, agendas and notes for you to refer to whenever you want to. You could also include any other electronic evidence of activities that you have carried out as part of your personal development.

Paper-based

When you attend training courses, there are likely to be handouts, paper copies of presentations and other documents that you may wish to refer to later. These can be filed in a paper-based system if not available electronically.

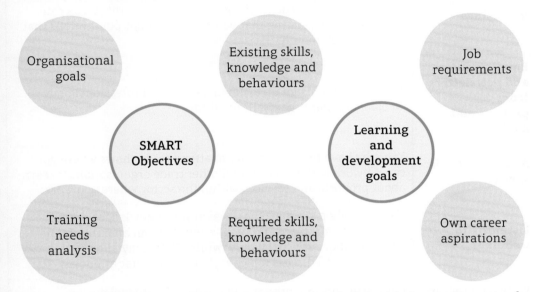

Figure 1: How do your own learning and development goals link with the requirements of your job?

Types of CPD activity

Formal training is not the only way in which you can undertake personal development. Table 2 details other possible forms of CPD activity.

Reading journals and magazines	You may have access to industry magazines or journals at work and read articles that improve your knowledge, or you may have a regular subscription. You can add this activity to your CPD record, detailing specific articles, if appropriate. Alternatively you can make one entry, stating that you receive regular publications that you read each month.
Email updates and newsletters from professional bodies	Check if you can sign up to email alerts on a professional body website for your organisation's sector.
Attending trade shows	You may have the opportunity to attend trade shows where you can network with suppliers and other trade organisations to learn about products and services within the sector where you work.
Listening to webinars	Webinars are a great way to develop your knowledge without leaving the workplace and require only a small amount of time. Some webinars are 'listen only' while others may allow you to participate and discuss topics with other webinar attendees.
Watching sector-related TV documentaries	Interesting documentaries and business-related television programmes can help you to develop your knowledge, skills and/or behaviours.
Business meetings	If you attend business meetings, there may be occasions when the agenda is related to staff training or you may learn something through the natural progression of the meeting. If any new knowledge or skills are genuinely gained and help you to develop, you should enter the details onto your CPD record.
Conversations	As part of your working day, you may have conversations with several different people, such as colleagues, suppliers, stakeholders and customers. Any significant learning gained from these conversations that are relevant to your personal development may be entered onto your CPD record.

Table 2: Can you think of other CPD activities?

When deciding what to enter onto your CPD record, ask: 'What have I learned?', 'How will this learning make a difference to my performance at work?', 'Is this learning relevant to my goals and/or career aspirations?'. If you have learned something new that is going to, or has improved your knowledge, skills and/or behaviours, and it is related to your job or career aspirations, then you should include it in your CPD record.

Appropriate range of learning activities

> When putting together a PDP to determine your learning and development activities, you should ensure your choices are appropriate and make the best use of the time and resources available to you.

Link to the standard

CPD Professional Discussion band 1.3

Formal learning and development, such as training programmes and/or qualifications, can be costly and mean you must be released from your job to attend off the job training. This will be an additional cost to the business, particularly if cover is required while you are away. Another example is supplier training; you should establish the content of the training by asking yourself: 'Is it going to be useful to my development, or is the supplier using the training to advertise its products or services?'

It is essential that you only take up learning and development opportunities that will have an impact on your performance and that meet the needs, goals and strategy of your organisation; see figure 2. There will be other appropriate forms of CPD that you can identify through discussion with your line manager when having one-to-one meetings. Each of these should be carefully considered to ensure that you have an appropriate range of learning activities to meet your development needs and goals that you have agreed.

Behaviours

Takes responsibility – Drive to achieve in all aspects of work. Demonstrates resilience and accountability.

Inclusive – Seeks views of others.

Agile – Flexible to the needs of the organisation.

Identified learning and development goals	Range of agreed development activities	New knowledge, skills and behaviours

Figure 2: What are your learning and development goals?

Making the right choice

Link to the standard

CPD Professional Discussion band 1.4

When deciding on which learning and development activities to undertake you should consider several factors.

The learning and development activities you undertake should relate to all or the most relevant of the following:

Behaviours

Takes responsibility – Drive to achieve in all aspects of work. Demonstrates resilience and accountability.
Inclusive – Seeks views of others.
Agile – Flexible to the needs of the organisation.

- your identified learning and development goals
- your personal objectives that have been agreed with your line manager
- the requirements of the job
- your career aspirations
- organisational objectives
- organisational strategy.

There should be sound reasoning for the choices you have made for the learning and development activities that you undertake and there should be a direct connection between them and how they will support the achievement of your learning and development goals and/or objectives.

Link to the standard

CPD Professional Discussion band 1.5, 1.6

Identifying what you have learned from your CPD activities

Following any learning and development activities you should be able to describe the knowledge, skills and/or behaviours you have gained. Table 3 includes questions you can ask yourself to organise your thoughts as to what you have learned and how you have developed your knowledge, skills and behaviours.

Knowledge	What new knowledge do you have? Why did you need to know this? How will it improve your performance at work? How can you use this knowledge to further improve your performance?
Skills	What new skills have you gained? How will these new skills be useful to you at work? What impact will these new skills have on your organisational goals and/or strategy? How will you ensure that you embed these new skills?
Behaviours	How will you change your behaviour? What impact will this have on your role as a team leader? How will you ensure that you embed these new behaviours? How will these new behaviours help you to develop and achieve your goals and/or career aspirations?

Table 3: What have you learned from your CPD activities?

Effectiveness of your CPD activities

Any learning and development activities that you undertake should result in you making a difference at work; see figure 3. It might be that you have learned a new skill to enable you to undertake a new role. You may now be able to operate a new piece of machinery or have increased your knowledge in order to become more effective. You might have received training on how changing your behaviour will enable you to think about how you do things and how you can challenge your thinking at work.

New skill
Using coaching techniques and coaching models when working with individual team members.

New knowledge
Understanding how coaching techniques work and how changing my behaviours will improve my skills.

New behaviour
Give my team members time to reflect and talk through their options. Don't make assumptions.

Figure 3: In which ways are your learning and development activities making a difference to you at work?

You may also find that some activities incorporate a combination of all three elements in figure 3. For example, you may undertake training for a skill that requires you to know and understand the reasons behind this new skill. This also requires that you think differently as you start to embed the new skills and knowledge.

Self-assessment and seeking feedback from others will help you to establish the effectiveness of the learning and development activities you have undertaken. It will help you to identify any potential implications for future learning and development planning. Use table 4 to assess the effectiveness of your CPD activities.

Self-assessment	Feedback from others
How do my learning and development activities align with my objectives/goals and those of my organisation? How will this new knowledge/skill/behaviour benefit me in my role? How will it make me more effective? How will I know that I am more effective? What opportunities will I have to practise what I have learned? What potential implications are there for future learning and development activities?	Who can I obtain feedback from to confirm that my new knowledge/skill/behaviour is making me more effective? What feedback have I received to confirm this? What evidence is there from others that I am making a difference?

Table 4: Answer these questions to assess the effectiveness of your CPD activities

You may receive feedback from your line manager during an appraisal or one-to-one meeting, which may be recorded onto an official document such as a PDP. The PDP is a useful document that you can refer to throughout the year to ensure that you stay focused on important elements in your learning and development and record your achievements as you recognise further development requirements.

Applying your new knowledge, skills and behaviours and the impact on your everyday work practice

Link to the standard

CPD Professional Discussion band 1.7, 1.8

Behaviours

Takes responsibility – Drive to achieve in all aspects of work. Demonstrates resilience and accountability.
Agile – Flexible to the needs of the organisation.

Nothing will change unless you continuously practise the new skills, knowledge and behaviours you have learned through following the activities you have undertaken. It may not feel natural in the beginning, but the more you practise a new skill or behaviour, the more it will become familiar until eventually you will use these skills and behaviours without thinking about them.

There are four stages of competence, as explained in figure 4.

Unconscious incompetence	**Conscious incompetence**	**Conscious competence**	**Unconscious competence**
At this first stage you do not have the competence levels required to be able to undertake your role competently.	You then become aware of what knowledge, skills and behaviours are required to become competent.	You start to learn and apply the knowledge, skills and behaviours, but must think about what you are doing continuously.	You are now able to perform competently, consistently and naturally as you reach your learning and development goals.

Figure 4: Which stage of competence have you reached?

Once you have reached the unconscious competence stage, you should ask yourself how you have applied your new knowledge, skills and behaviours in your everyday work practice and what evidence you have to confirm this. For example, this evidence could be in the form of reports detailing targets and deadlines you have met, notes from one-to-one meetings you have had with your line manager or a witness testimony from a credible person you have worked with.

This will then lead you to be able to complete a rational evaluation of how your learning has affected your work performance and the potential impact it has on your organisational goals and/or strategy.

Summary

In this section you have learned about different aspects of continuous professional development (CPD) and how it is an important part of your learning and development at work. This section has covered:

- writing SMART objectives that relate to your CPD
- recording your CPD
- types of CPD activity
- identifying a range of relevant learning activities that you can record on a personal development plan
- recognising what you have learned from your CPD activities and how effective they have been
- applying any new knowledge, skills and/or behaviours that you develop for your role as a team leader.

Activities

▶ **Activity 1**

Think about the learning and development goals you have been given and write at least three SMART objectives that will help you to achieve them.

OR

If you already have objectives set, revisit them and check that they are SMART.

Then write a statement to cover the following:

1. how the objectives set are SMART objectives and how you will know when you have achieved your goals

2. the relationship between your objectives and your job requirements and organisational goals

3. the relationship between your objectives and your career aspirations.

▶ **Activity 2**

Locate your record of learning and development activities (CPD).

OR

If you do not have a record of CPD, create one.

Then identify five different learning activities you have undertaken and against each explain:

1. how each activity links to a specific objective and will support the achievement of your identified goals

2. the learning you have gained from that activity

3. why you chose each of the learning and development activities.

▶ **Activity 3**

Think about the knowledge, skills and behaviours that you have developed throughout your apprenticeship programme and answer the following:

1. What new knowledge have you gained?

2. What new skills have you developed?

3. How have your behaviours changed?

▶ **Activity 4**

Using your CPD record, identify five different learning activities and reflect on their effectiveness by answering the following:

1. Which activity has had the most impact on you at work and why?

2. Which activity has had the least impact on you and why?

3. Do you still have gaps in your knowledge, skills or behaviours?

4. If so, what are these gaps and how will you plan to meet them?

▶ **Activity 5**

Think about the learning and development you have undertaken throughout your apprenticeship and answer the following:

1. How have you applied new knowledge in your team leading role?

2. How have you used new skills?

3. How have your behaviours changed so that you are more effective in your role?

4. What feedback from others have you received to confirm that you have applied your new knowledge, skills and behaviours competently?

▶ **Activity 6**

Using your organisational goals and/or strategy as your benchmark, answer the following:

1. How has your learning affected your performance at work?

2. What impact has this had on your organisational goals and/or strategy?

3. What potential impact could your learning have on your organisational goals and/or strategy?

Topic consolidation

▶ Test yourself

1. How would you rate your ability to manage your professional development?

   ☐ excellent
   ☐ good
   ☐ requires improvement
   ☐ inadequate

2. A TNA will help you to:

   ☐ establish your learning and development needs
   ☐ write SMART objectives
   ☐ understand what your organisation requires of you
   ☐ record your CPD.

3. A CPD activity must be:

   ☐ a formal learning and development activity
   ☐ any activity where you have learned something new
   ☐ only linked to your career aspirations
   ☐ authorised by your manager.

4. You know your CPD activities have been effective in your role when:

   ☐ you receive a pay rise
   ☐ you move into the conscious competence stage
   ☐ your team like you
   ☐ you make a difference at work.

5. When you are unaware of the competence levels required to do your job you are:

   ☐ unconsciously competent
   ☐ consciously incompetent
   ☐ consciously competent
   ☐ unconsciously competent.

6. How would you rate your ability to apply new knowledge and skills in your role?

   ☐ excellent
   ☐ good
   ☐ requires improvement
   ☐ inadequate

7. The M in SMART stands for:

   ☐ measurable
   ☐ mean
   ☐ meaningful
   ☐ maintain

8. Business meetings can be a part of CPD activity when:

   ☐ the meeting is informal
   ☐ you learn something new
   ☐ the agenda is full
   ☐ it is a formal meeting.

9. You know new learning has been effective and should be entered onto your CPD record when:

☐ it meets the organisational objectives
☐ the activity is at least four hours long
☐ there are others learning with you
☐ there is a formal programme of learning.

10. A self-assessment activity might include:

☐ obtaining feedback from your manager
☐ observing how others learn
☐ identifying how your learning aligns with your objectives
☐ demonstrating new behaviours.

Glossary

Adhering – follow and be in support of something

Adversely – in a way that is harmful or prevents achievement

Agenda – the list of items that will be discussed during the meeting

Amicably – in a friendly and peaceful manner

Appraisal/performance management review – an ongoing process to review and evaluate the performance of employees

Aspirations – things that you hope to achieve

Auditing – the systematic and in-depth checking, analysis and evaluation to check for accuracy

Autonomy – a level of freedom given to an individual, that enables them to take decisions

Benchmark – a point of reference by which something may be compared

Benchmarking – measuring the organisation's performance against the best organisations in the industry

Bias – favouritism towards or against something

Body language – the use of movement or posture to communicate attitudes and feelings

Brainstorming – developing and analysing creative ideas

Budgets – estimate or plan income or expenditure during a certain period of time

Bureaucracy – a system for controlling processes with rigid and inflexible rules

Cash flow – the money coming into and going out of the business

Catalyst – a person or event that causes a change

Chair – the person responsible for leading and controlling a meeting

Coachee – the individual being coached

Cohesion – united and working together

Cohesive – united and working together effectively

Collaboration – working together to achieve a shared goal

Compliance – adherence to laws, policies and procedures

Conflict – a serious argument or disagreement

Constructive criticism – well-reasoned and valid feedback, based on both positives and negatives

Cooperation – two or more people working together

Corporation tax – tax on a company's profits

Costs of sales – the cost of stock or material costs

Critical path analysis – involves analysing the different stages of a project to find the shortest sequence of stages to completing the project – the 'critical path'

Deficiency – failing or shortcoming

Delegate – to trust someone to do a job for you

Deliverables – products or services produced as the output of a project

Demographics – the breakdown of a country's population into different characteristic groups such as gender, age or income

Direct costs – those costs that can be directly attributed to the production process such as the cost of raw materials or stock

Directive – an order or command

Discipline – the identification of unacceptable behaviour or conduct by a supervisor or manager, requiring improvements in behaviour

Discriminatory behaviour – the actions or behaviours that discriminate unfairly based on race, gender, etc.

Economic growth – an increase in the number of goods and services produced by the country over time

Emotional intelligence – being aware of and able to express your emotions while controlling them effectively

Empathy – the ability to share and understand other people's feelings

Employee turnover – the number of employees leaving the organisation

Empowerment – giving power and control to individuals to make decisions and act themselves

Escalation – to increase the intensity or seriousness of a situation

Expenditure – money spent, or going out of the organisation

Extrinsic – external or coming from the outside

Facilitator – a person who helps another find an answer to a problem or to do something more easily through guidance or supervision

Formal communication – communication via the official channels in the organisation

Goals – long-term targets you want to achieve

Governance – the policies, processes and procedures that exist to satisfy the requirements of the government and statutory compliance requirements

Grievance – complaint about unfair treatment in the workplace

Ground rules – principles of behaviours and actions that both parties agree to

Hierarchy – a system where items are organised and ranked in order of importance, status or authority

Inception – the starting point of a project or plan

Income – money that is generated, or coming into the organisation

Indirect costs – costs that cannot be attributed directly to the production process such as administration or marketing

Inflation – the general rise in the average price level in a country over time

Informal communication – communication through unofficial channels such as rumours, gossip and chats at the coffee machine

Innovation – a new and creative idea, device or process

Interpersonal relationships – connections or interactions that are developed between two or more people who share common goals in the workplace

Intrinsic – the essential part of something

Key performance indicators – a set of performance measurements used in an organisation that reflect the company's values and objectives

Leadership – the act of leading and motivating for a common goal

Marketing – the activity of buying, selling, distributing and promoting products

Medium – a means to use when doing something

Milestones – significant stages in developing a plan or project

Minutes – detailed notes that are taken during formal meetings to provide a record of what was discussed

Mitigate – to reduce the severity of a situation

Mitigation – an action to reduce the severity or seriousness of something

Negotiation – formal discussion between people who have different aims or intentions, during which they try to reach an agreement

Needs analysis – a process to establish the training and/or development needs of an individual

Objectives – measurable steps you must take to achieve a strategy or goal

Organisational culture – a system of shared assumptions, values and beliefs which govern behaviours within an organisation

Perpetrator – an individual who carries out a harmful or illegal act

Personal development plan (PDP) – a plan outlining the objectives, activities and support of personal development

Personal skills – skills that help you understand yourself and develop good self-awareness

PESTLE analysis – analytical tool used to consider all the external factors that affect an organisation, project or idea

Productivity – the measure of the productive output of an individual, team, machine or period of time

Project life cycle – the four stage process that can be followed by project managers when completing a project

Qualifying disclosures – information that an employee is reasonably expected to disclose to their employers regarding past, present or pending behaviour or offences

Rationale – reasons or a logical basis for a course of action

Rationalised – attempt to explain or justify

Reflection – giving thought or consideration to an idea or action

Remedial – to correct something that is wrong or improve a bad situation

Service level agreements – contracts between a service provider and end user that set the level of service expected

Skills audit – process used to identify gaps in your skills

SMART – an acronym for objectives that are **s**pecific, **m**easurable, **a**chievable, **r**ealistic and **t**ime-sensitive

Social skills – skills that we use to interact and communicate effectively with other people

Soft skills – transferable or professional skills

Stakeholders – individuals or groups that have an interest in the organisation or project

Statutory – something that is required or expected

Subordinate – someone who is junior or an assistant to the team leader

Training needs analysis – a process to identify the gap between the existing skills, knowledge and behaviours of an individual and the skills, knowledge and behaviours required to do their job

Triangulation – using two or more sources of information to check that it is accurate

Tribunal – a board or panel set up to settle a dispute

Verbal communication – the sharing of information between individuals by speech

Whistleblowing – reporting the behaviour or actions of wrongdoing to the employer or relevant organisation

Working practices – the ways in which tasks and activities are undertaken at work

Workshops – meetings to hold intensive discussion and analysis of a project or idea

Work-specific skills – the skills related to your specific job role

Index